THE SPIRITUALITY OF JOY

OTHER BOOKS AND WRITINGS BY DR. JAMES E. McREYNOLDS

A Baptist History
A Behavioral View of Boundary Transgressions in Therapeutic Relationships
A Church of Joy: History of Washington Chapel United Methodist Church
Acts: A Bible Study Workbook
Adjusting Your Attitude: The Book of Numbers
Advent: A Time for Joy
Advent Devotional Book of the Christian Church in Nebraska, 2010
Advent Devotionals 1997
Advent Devotionals 1996
Advent Devotionals for Christian Church in Nebraska 2008
Advent Worship With the Faith Church Family
A Glimmer of Hope Despite Despair: Teaching of Lamentations
A Good Marriage Begins With Me
A Guide to Preaching: Lay Leadership Training
A Journey of Spiritual Joy: Joyful Conversations Guide
A King and a Pair of Queens: The Story of Esther
A Living Lesson on Forgiveness: Philemon
All Glory to God: A Commentary on First Corinthians 3:5-6:10
A Love Your Children Can Share Forever
American Vignettes: A Collection of Footnotes to History
America's Number One Drug Problem
A New Attitude
A Night With People of the Cross
Annie at Seven-Oh! (contributor)
An Ounce of Prevention: A Church-Based Program of Drug Abuse Prevention
A Treasury of Modern Poets
Alcoholics Are God's Children Too
Anointed Soul, Spiritual Rocks
Apprentice Shepherds for a Modern Age
A Psychology of Wellness
Arrows in Your Quiver
A Vision Quest for Maturing in Christ
A Visionquesting Tool for Understanding Ourselves
Baptism: Truth or Tradition
Because My Love Holds No Strings
Behold: A Biblical Understanding of God's New Creation
Bible Chronicles Before Christ: Old Testament Highlights
Bible in Pocket, Gun in Hand
Bible Introduction 101
Bible Pictures of Water: Special Lent Sermons

Design for Personal Spiritual Visionquest
Deuteronomy: The Law That Delivers
Developmental Disabilities and Borderline Personality Disorder
Difficult Children
Discovering the Church as a Disciplinary Force for Joy
Divorce on Trial
Don't Mistake Meekness for Weakness: A Commentary on II Corinthians
Dramatic Feelings During Holy Days
Elijah
Elisha
Empty Tomb: Lenten Study Series
Encountering the Eternal: The Letters of John
Encyclopedia of Southern Baptists: Volume III
Enrichment: A New Blueprint for Marriage
Everything You Always Wanted to Know About Angels
Experiencing Easter
Ezekiel: Visionquests of the Restoration of Israel
Faithfulness in the Church Before the Lord's Return: I and II Thessalonians
Faithful to the Final Bell: A Commentary on II Thessalonians
Faith Journeys When You Are at Wit's End
Faith Makes a Difference
Families and History of Sullivan County, Tennessee, 1779-1992
Family Guidance and Transition for Life
Family Guidance 101: Communication
Fellows Yearbook 2000
Fighting for the Faith: Jude
Final Visionquests
Finding Joy in Perseverance
Finding Unity in the Body of Christ: A Commentary on I Corinthians 12:12-16:24
Fired Up or Burned Out: Connections to Ignite Passion and Productivity
First Christian Church Annual Report 2006
First Christian Church Annual Report 2007: Our Story During 2007
First Christian Church Annual Report 2008: Our Church of Contagious Joy
Flames, Lions, Visions, and Dreams: The Challenge of Daniel
Food for the Soul: Lenten Meditations for Those in Prison
Gaining God's Grace in Galatians
Genesis of the Grace of God
Getting Angry Makes Me Mad
Getting Up and Going Again
Getting Up Getting You Down
God's Design for Leadership: A Commentary on First Samuel, chapters 1-11
God Gives His Answer: A Commentary on the Book of Malachi

Inspirations: Prayers for Hearth and Home
Interpretation of Dreams on the Spiritual Journey
Interpretation of the Sermon on the Mount
Irresistible Grace: Healing Grace for a Lifetime
Isaiah: Trusting God in Turbulent, Troubled Times
Islam: The Awful Challenge to Christian Faith
It's Hard to Say Goodbye
James: Faith That Works
James McReynolds' Dictionary of Illustrations and Outlines
Jeremiah: The Reluctant Prophet
Jesus and the People: Proclaiming the Kingdom of God (Matthew 11-20)
Jesus Christ Is Lord
Jesus Sets Us Free: A Parish Religious Education Series
Jonah: God's Global Reach
Joseph Under the McReyscope
Joshua: The Lord Is Salvation
Joy Beyond Survival: A New Spirituality
Joy Beyond the Walls of This World
Joy in the Mourning: Preaching Joy at a Funeral
Judges: People Seeking Independence From God
Judgment and Deliverance: A Commentary on the Book of Micah
Keeping Our Resolutions
Keeping the Home Fires Burning
Key to Spirituality: A Commentary on Colossians, chapters 1-2
King of the Jews, King of Glory (Matthew 21-28)
Last Passages for Persons With Disabilities
Learning to Live Drug Free
Legacy of David: A Commentary on II Samuel, chapters 18-24
Let All the People: Visionquests From the Children's Sermon Box
Liturgical Preaching
Living by Faith: In Wrath Remember Mercy: Bible Teaching of Habakkuk
Living in God's Embrace: The Practice of Intimacy
Living in Love
Living With Olympic Faith
Looking Through a Father's Soul
Love for the First Conflicted Church at Corinth: I Corinthians
Love That Lasts a Lifetime
Love Is the Bottom Line
Love: A Cornerstone of Faith
Luke: A Spiritual Commentary
Making Relaxation Work for You
Making Sense Out of Adolescence

Presbyterian New Members Class
Presbyterian Preaching: Shenandoah Sermons
Prescription for Today: Meditations for the Sick
Pressing On to Maturity: Part II of First Thessalonians Commentary
Prophets and Kings in the Kingdom of Israel
Proverbs and Refreshing Relationships
Provision or Penalty, Blessing or Judgment
Psalms in Reflection
Psychology of Love: The Real Stuff
Public Petitions: Powerful Positive Prayer
Putting Our Faith to Work: A Commentary on the Book of James
Queen of the Epistles: A Commentary on the Book of Ephesians
Quest for Guidance When the Bible Doesn't Say
Quest for Joy: Life Beyond Pleasure and Profit
Quick Crowdbreakers and Games for Youth Groups
Reaching the Sunset Years
Refreshing Relationships
Remember Your Redeemer: Sermons From a Student Pastor
Rendering to Caesar: A Biblical Perspective on Government
Resisting Our Resentments
Resurrection Joy: The Laughter of God
Resurrection People
Revealing the Riches of the Revelation
Revelation of John: The Lamb Wins
Rock-a-Bye Baby: Understanding Family Stress
Ruth Under the McReyscope
Sanctified Suffering: A Commentary on I Peter
Searching and Finding Mega Joy
Seeking for the Kingdom: A Bible Commentary on the Book of Haggai
Sermons on the Ten Commandments
Sermons to Create a Christ Centered Church
Sermons to the Church on Evangelism and Christian Witness
Serving the Least of These: Caring for Those Living With Mental Disorders
Serving in the Vineyard in 2009
Setting Our Minds on the Spirit
Seven Parables of the Savior
Seventh and Eighth Century Minor Prophets: Nahum, Habakkuk, Zephaniah, Obadiah
Sexual Attraction and Moral Choices: The Story of Ruth
Sexual Intimacy: Song of Solomon
Sexually Abused Children in Foster Care
Simple Spirituality

The Desert Sounds of Spirituality (Psalms 50-90)
The Drama of Deliverance
The Epistle of Paul the Apostle to the Philippians
The Essence of Evangelism
The Expositional Eulogy: Teaching Pastoral Preaching for Funeral Sermons
The Filling of Empty Vacuums
The Fruit of the Spirit: Joy to the World
The Gift of Prayer
The Good News of All God's People
The Gospel of God's Grace: Romans
The Gospel of Joy According to Luke
The Gospel of Luke and a Theology of Suffering and Disability
The Gospel of Mark the Evangelist
The Integrity of the New Covenant: II Corinthians
The Intensity of Joy
The Journey of the Human Soul
The Journey Into Christmas: A Quest for Joy
The Joy Factor
The Joy of Finding the Changeless God in Our Changing Society
The Joy of Knowing God
The Joy of Managing Your Anger
The Joy of the Lord Is My Strength: Nehemiah
The Ladder to Trouble
The Languages of Love
The Many Faces of Adolescent Depression
The McReynolds' Family: Who's Who in America
The Mighty Power of God: A Study of Daniel
The Ministry of the Church
The Peer Counselor's Pocket Book
The Person and Work of Jesus in the Gospel of Mark
The Power of Love in the Healthy Family
The Promised King: The Gospel According to Matthew
The Pursuit of Happiness: Philippians
The Recovery of God's House
The Return of Judah: Joel, Haggai, Zechariah, and Malachi
The Road Best Traveled Is Without Anger
The Road Less Traveled to Joy
The Seven Habits of Highly Effective Churches
The Scent of Joy
The Story of Joseph
The Symbolism of Our Faith
The Teacher and His Students (Matthew 5-10)

Contact Visionquests for Joy for speaking engagements:

Dr. James McReynolds
404 North 4th Street
ELMWOOD NE 68349-6022
Phone 402-994-2266
Email: joyquest@windstream.net

The Spirituality of Joy

THE LEAST DISCUSSED
HUMAN EMOTION

Dr. James E. McReynolds

Minister of Joy to the World

2011

Parson's Porch Books

Cleveland, Tennessee

Parson's Porch Books
121 Holly Trail Road, NW
Cleveland, Tennessee 37311

The Spirituality of Joy: The Least Discussed Human Emotion
© 2011 by James E. McReynolds. All rights reserved.
Published 2011.
Printed in the United States of America.
ISBN 978-1-936912-10-0

To order additional copies of this book, contact:

Parson's Porch Books
1-423-475-7308
www.parsonsporchbooks.com

This book is affectionately dedicated to

Ethan Sean Coffin

May Ethan always have his radiant smile. And if he ever loses it for a time, may he and we know that a joy will fall from heaven to bring it back.

—Grandpapa Jim

TABLE OF CONTENTS

INTRODUCTION

This book is lovingly dedicated to my grandson Ethan. Ethan holds a continuous smile with his searching blue eyes. He finds joy in so many things. Whenever I find myself living in a valley time, I know I am recovering when I get my smile back.

I completed the initial writing of this book in the summer of 2009. Then, the hard drive on my computer fizzled out. I lost five years of work including my book on joy.

My Recovery, Inc. support group helped me see this trauma as a triviality in life. I endorsed myself for making the effort to get a new hard drive. I came into his world with nothing and I'll go out with the same. I bore the discomfort of starting over. John Killinger, my mentor and friend, said the next attempt would be fresh and better. Linda McReynolds, my daughter, had saved some of the outline and early writing. God might have wanted something in this final version that will tap into your joy instinct.

My title for this book comes out of my life. During a School of Practical Christianity session, Norman Vincent Peale, the famous positive thinking pastor, anointed me as "minister of joy to the world."

Writing this book has brought me closer to God. Advertisements of things that are supposed to bring us joy and any earthly achievements cannot compare to being aware of joys in life. Jane Pauley thinks of joy as "the things falling out of heaven theory." I know Ethan and Linda came from heaven. I see it in their eyes and their warm smiles. I just bet you see it in your children and grandchildren too.

Finding the joy of eternal union with God including perfect beauty and majesty demonstrates to me that the good things in this life are simply a dress rehearsal for the next. Death is a curtain call as *jouissance* is a French word for "exceeding joy," or "passionate joy."

Joy comes from the same Latin word as rejoicing. In my world with all the love God has shown to my family and me, I have known this exceeding joy. I know that in my wife Laurel Ann and through friends and family, I have known a harbinger of the most intense and perfect joy of heaven.

When Linda, my daughter, was born, I could not contain the love and the joy I felt and still do. Along the hills and valleys, the rocky and tumultuous paths, which I have described in an earlier book, *Dancing With Bipolar Bears: Living in Joy Despite Illness*, my family and I often used humor to lighten the struggles. Our joy in the face of worldly obstacles is living proof of the promises of God that our sorrow will be turned into laughter. Passionate joy is the opposite of depression.

My paraphrase of John 16:22 reads, "So you are now in the valleys of anguish!

"But I will see you again, and your hearts will hold jouissance, and no one will take your joy away." Because we lack passion we lack joy.

Joy is proof that God lives in us. Still, Christians hunger for love and become depressed, stressed out, and sad. Examples of faithful yet human saints can bring us closer to God who is all joy. I have learned from them. My old friend John Claypool called us "fellow strugglers."

God's abundance is unlimited. We can drink from the inexhaustible source of joy, and when we do, we'll know perfect peace.

PRACTICAL APPLICATION

Before you begin reading, take out a piece of paper. Draw a line horizontally across the middle of the page. At the extreme left side write on the line "birth." Then write at five-year intervals the hills and valleys of your life to date. Write hills in the upper space and write a word or two to indicate your valleys in the lower space.

I

JOY AND OUR LIFE PURPOSE

The Secret of joy in work is contained in one word: excellence. To know how to do something well is to enjoy it.

— Pearl S. Buck

B UILDING A WEALTH OF JOY in a world starved for love is our life purpose. In rich nations such as the United States of America, little is known about joy. Joy is the least discussed human emotion.

Surveys reveal that in the years of American research, there have been more than 50,000 professional papers written on depression, and less than 50 on joy or happiness.

Psychotherapists integrate most any topic or theory into new theories of psychotherapy, but we are in total darkness about the qualities that make life most worth living.

His Holiness the Dalai Lama and a therapist, Howard Cutler, wrote a book titled *The Art of Happiness* in 1998. Millions read it. Tenzin Gyatso (the current Dalai Lama) assured us that the purpose of life is to seek joy and the motion of life is toward happiness.

Evidence shows that the brain can change direction. Recovery groups say "move your muscles" and the brain will respond to the muscles. We have more control of emotions, including joy, than we have ever believed. We have ceded investigative research on joy to advertising specialists, travel agents, novelists, or therapists.

So we grew indifferent to claims about mind-body connections, but now we need to explore this least discussed human emotion to create a more blessing-filled life.

Building a wealth of joy means to eliminate the mass starvation of love

Eliminating the causes of love starvation will create an atmosphere for mourning and suffering. Joy came in our historical mourning through the emancipation of slaves.

Women's suffrage, civil rights, withdrawal from war-making, eliminating apartheid in South Africa, and living with the mentally ill without stigma and discrimination finally brought a climate of joy to our world. With painful mourning, the overclass oppressors and the underclass oppressed found joy then and now.

Jouissance is a French word coined by Jacques Lacan, a psychoanalyst. It means radical or excessive joy. Lacan's word means *radical* in the real sense of the word, meaning "going to the roots." Radical joy goes to the roots of who we are.

Excessive joy, a dancing joy came in the mourning with different values, a different view of reality, and humankind achieved a quantum leap in a wealth of joy.

Many were taught not to dance at all. Some were burned while dancing for pleasure, for love, for security, for validation, and all the while they already had a treasure within that included not only those good things but better things involving an ever widening circle of people who rushed to draw out their share of *jouissance* until it has now the possibility of engulfing all humanity.

Something must have taught us how to be blind from birth. So we just can't enjoy a Nebraska sunset, a red rose, clean sheets wind-blown on the clothesline, a basketball swished into the net, or a piece of art.

Expecting us to smell the roses, to cease the anger, to slow down, to take off the false masks, is like expecting a blind person to suddenly see like others see. There is one difference: eventually we can do it.

To know *passionate joy* we must live as if the world depended on what we do, while laughing at ourselves for thinking that what we do will make any difference. Einstein said, "If at first the idea is not absurd, it has no hope."

We must stop fussing about which way is right or wrong. If we cannot build a wealth of joy, we will have allowed the extinction of human beings. Building joy in our world starved for love is the only hope for preventing the horrors, evidenced by 9/11 from snowballing out of control.

All emotions, negative and positive, represent an energized thought-based pattern that overpowers us. Emotions and thoughts feed on each other. By dwelling on a problem, a life situation, event, or another person that is perceived as the cause of the feeling, our thoughts give energy to our emotions.

All human emotions are really one undifferentiated emotion. Guilt feeds on fear that feeds on anger that feeds on anxiety. The harder our minds struggle not to feel and act out our feelings, the harder our minds struggle to get rid of the painful emotions, the greater the pain. The demons in our mind cannot find a solution, nor can they allow you to find a solution. The pattern is much like a fire chief trying to find an arsonist when the arsonist is that fire chief.

Jouissance from the sufferings brought by negative emotions will only be found when human beings stop finding their sense of self from their negative thoughts. The negative emotions become the mafia of the mind. Joy comes when a gap occurs in the stream of our thought life. These gaps are rare. They come when the demons of the mind stop spinning. Sometimes joy arrives in an encounter with surprising beauty or a creation. And within that time of stillness, there comes peace. Joy comes in a brief moment of time. These experiences are rare, short-lived, as the demons in the mind resume their noise-making activity.

Hate cannot eliminate hate, only love can make joy possible.

Love is the spirit of our highest intelligence, our inspiration, intuition, creativity, empathy, and joy. Love is the spirit that will die joyfully to keep others alive.

We must care deeply about building joy. Small helpings of love generate limited amounts of joy. Big acts of love bring an atmosphere for big amounts of joy. We have allowed our world to be committed not to building joy, but to create a different measure of wellbeing, namely pleasure, material wealth, power, status, comfort, and security.

Mother Theresa observed "a poverty of spirit in the west." Martin Luther King warned us of our "poverty of conscience." Psychologists Maslow, Kohlberg, and Ciskszentmihalyi estimate that less than one person in 100,000 lives a life with moments of joy, regardless of their socio-economic advantages or disadvantages.

Jouissance as excessive joy comes through the mourning. Gandhi said, "Do you know that I am never as joyful as when I am suffering for others?" Martin Luther King told us, "A person is not fit to live until he knows what he will die for." Viktor

Frankl observed that while others might be suffering horribly from abject conditions, individuals in pursuits of great meaning transcend their suffering."

In a loving covenant community, we must practice the skills. People can gather in groups to find some of the skills, thought patterns, activities, and new ways of dealing with feelings. Understanding radical joy helps us understand why we struggle, what we are struggling against, and how we can take charge of our struggle.

Connected people can share their joys, multiplying those joys. Even if your sky is heavily overcast, the sun has not disappeared. There is more joy, love, and peace on the other side of the dark clouds. Shared suffering is half the suffering. Shared joy is double joy.

The German words for joy and friends are almost identical. *Freude* is joy. *Freunde* is friend. One has an "n" in it, the other does not. When we share our joy, we create friendship and community.

When we have good news, we call a friend because friends have this gift of totally delighting in whatever we share. There is never envy or competition. We need to become somebody like that to build a wealth of joy.

Baby boomers whose fathers fought in World War II are at risk of being bankrupt of joy. All wars have an aftermath of clinical depression, post-traumatic stress disorder, bipolarity, and other DSM-IV diagnoses. So we'll have to treat millions from today's wars. These disorders are the second most costly disease in the United States. Billions are spent on unnecessary medical care, lost production at work, shortened life spans, and one in every eight Americans suffers.

We are creating pain now. Some of this pain comes from our past, perhaps eons past but it still lives on in our minds, our bodies, and our souls.

Stopping the present pain and dissolving the past pain, this is our calling. Will we bring excessive joy, radical joy—*jouissance*—to our world? Will we be wounded healers? Will we listen to the words of pain? What will we do to fulfill our life purpose?

We all do our best to find these answers to the questions concerning our purpose. As much as we might like someone to point us in the correct direction, each of us has to discover our own way and take our own steps. Discovering our life purpose requires a series of decisions. Those decisions will take all kinds of forms and differing shapes and change at different times or transitions in our lives.

We might ask, "Where shall we work and what will be the nature of our work?" "Will we find our identity in being a single person, or should we search for a partner?" "Is this the right time for birthing a child, or would it be better to wait?" "Where should we live and what kind of lifestyle will be correct for us?" "What about my retirement years?" "What do we do with the remaining years as we become older?"

It is not easy to discover our purpose. Some of us may be standing at a crossroads at this time, wondering what we should do as we battle a question that keeps grabbing us by the throat. Should I leave or should I stay? Should I let go, or should I keep holding on? Should I speak up or should I remain silent? Should I wait it out, or should I take action? Should I take the risk, or should I play it safe? What should I do with my life? How do I make an impact on our world? Some have a purpose that will affect just a few people. Others will help thousands of persons. Just like in an orchestra, every player is equally important. The piccolo player and the first violinist are important to the music's orchestration.

We are here to make the world a better place. If we believe that we are not doing so, our inner self begins to nudge us. This nudging may take on the form of anxiety or a sense of time urgency. If we choose to ignore our intuitive nudging, we will feel empty and depressed. If we think other people are blocking out these directions, we will blame them. We may rage. We believe we have been ripped off. If we believe we have no talent, no qualifications to help the world, we collapse into depression with lack of self-esteem.

A university student about to graduate said, "I know that my purpose is to help human existence run a little smoother. I try to do my best with everyone I come in contact with, to help their lives appear easier and less difficult. I am here to guide people through life."

A hospital patient related, "I do not have to end my life. It's not mine to end. I have a purpose. I have not begun to finish what I came into this world to accomplish."

What could a penniless, sick, unknown woman do for all humanity? One way of knowing will come through that inner nudging. Negative things will continue to happen. Any one of us will have hills and valleys. Every experience is a learning time. Perhaps we do or fail to do things that are different from what we are supposed to be doing. We may get into such a negative pattern that we have to overcome our addiction to failure.

Many people can't even feel the inner nudging, that tap on the shoulder. We sabotage our happiness and capacity for joy. If we but listen, bit by bit, more blessings will come into our lives. We meet "angels" who will help us. Spiritual or part of humankind, these angels will give us information, even material support that we could never find by doing everything by ourselves. We will gradually, or suddenly, know our sense of purpose for our lives.

We will know moments of joy ourselves. But even more joy will be created as we add value to others in the world. Do not waste your time with people who don't want you around, or those who refuse to listen to you. Our purpose outlasts our jobs or our careers. If you can't work or have no formal job, go out and try doing something. Move your muscles. Do what you don't want to do. Make an effort. Plant a tree. Learn a foreign language. Learn how to paint. Attend conferences or seminars. Write a newspaper article. Learn how to build a house. Travel to a distant country before you think you're too old.

A professor at the University of Nebraska shared that only about ten per cent of the people took part in the American Revolutionary War.

When people first hear that inner nudging toward purpose, they might think their job is something grand like saving the planet. That sounds better than their nine–to–five, hit the clock jobs. So they quit. Of course, it is difficult to move any of your muscles, including your speech and thinking muscles, with no money. We can learn something of our purpose in any job. Any job adds value, even if it is just a paycheck. One vital secret of happiness is not doing what you love, but loving what you do. When you get that inner nudge, start figuring out how to add value to that job. There is a reason you're there. Add your value to your present job. Most jobs are really not contributing to the wealth of joy for the people on earth. Some people are making money from money. The money is moved from one desk to another. Perhaps you can visualize your life purpose in your spare time.

Many people never find a fit, a comfortable niche. Either they don't stick with one job very long, or they just can't please employers. We can't afford to give up. When our muscles move, the waves go out. Suddenly, new opportunities appear. Some people become bored with what they are doing, so they go after some new things, perhaps in greener pastures. Trouble is, the waves go out again, to either side of their muscle movements. This could never stop for them.

And for some people, that's not always negative. It is a learning experience to do new things. But we end up going in circles, frustrated. To master any job takes time. If we aren't willing to stick to a job where we are, we will never find purpose.

We need to build a network of contacts, information, expertise, and wealth to make as effective a difference as we would have if we had stayed in one direction for a longer time. Would we be best to have had one job for 50 years or 50 jobs in 50 years?

Just cocoon for a while and discover a purposeful job that adds value and that you really enjoy. And then choose to commit to stick with that position for a long period of time.

Life Purpose: Our Reason for Living

Our personal life purpose involves a particular characteristic, vocation, or talent that we develop in life. Patience or compassion may be your purpose. Our international or global purpose involves discovering, developing, and using our talents and interests to help other people. Work out what you are nudged into doing. As well as doing work that provides money for you, you might find yourself doing work that earns no monetary reward. The blessings will follow you in other ways, and sometimes in the form of money as well.

Finding our life's purpose, our reason for living, is crucial for happiness and joy. The search for a design, an identity, is perceived by many researchers in psychology as the number one drive within our personality. We want to know there is a reason for our life. We know that happiness is fleeting. Joy is time-limited. Unless we understand who we are and believe in our life direction, we will find ourselves overwhelmed by the bumps in the road of life. Life will be a desperate search for identity and purpose.

All our life experience is relevant, shaping us for our life mission. Growth is transpiring to see that all experiences can lead to good, even failures. From the very things we perceive as curses, can bring positive blessings that can help give reason and direction to our lives. We might ask, "How is it possible to find joy when we have a bad end of life's proverbial stick? We want to know the difficulties we suffer while in our valleys are for a reason.

Some of us are afraid of making mistakes. We fear other people's evaluation and opinion of us. The reason we don't just get out into life and move our muscles is our fear of making more mistakes. We learn by making mistakes.

When a baby makes its first efforts to walk the child stands up, and then falls down. No little one thinks, "I'm so embarrassed. I'll never try that again." We know that children stand up, fall down, stand up, fall down, and the baby keeps on keeping on until there is success at walking. Most of us can walk, so we have been through this.

Somewhere along life's way, our ego and the fear of other people's opinions got in the way. People start thinking they should never make a mistake. The only way to achieve that kind of goal is to do nothing. So some people choose to do nothing. The magic dies.

Who invented the light bulb? It was Thomas Edison. How many mistakes did he make before he succeeded? Some have quoted more than 10,000 mistakes. He found that many ways that it didn't work.

Kentucky Fried Chicken founder Colonel Sanders didn't have a dollar to his name when at age 65, he knocked on 1,009 doors before somebody agreed to buy his recipe and give him a royalty on every piece sold.

Joy can take root wherever it is planted. This planting is painful, dark, and scary. Tragedy plants in the negative ground. Being in a dark, deep hole is frightening, but with the sunlight's warmth and the gentle cleansing rains, life begins to flower and bear fruit again. Accepting all the circumstances of life frees us to bloom where we have been planted.

Searching for Life's Why and Our Purpose

Finding the answer to "Why am I here?" involves the recognition that every part of your life has a purpose. This insight frees us from appreciating the growing times, training times. Joy bubbles from recognizing our lives are filled with talents that can change the world. We can be bound to the valleys in our lives or we can soar with enthusiasm above our tethered cords.

Our personal truth is that we don't have to search the "whys." We are responsible for growing where we are. Roadblocks to our understanding how we can use our gifts and talents include our hurtful pasts, unhealthy comparisons, compulsive problems, bad marriages, or rebellious children. Some of us run all over the world seeking a geographical cure. We must decide to be happy wherever we are. We cannot afford to permit our hectic lives, commitments, busy schedules, or failures to take us down in the valley. No person can make us happy or unhappy.

All of our emotions are normal, good, and natural. Happiness is accepting all of them into our lives and saying that we enjoy living and we are grateful just to be alive.

Balance Between Reason and Emotion

Searching for life's purpose involves a balance between reason and emotion. Difficulties that dominate the valleys in life strengthen our emotional power over reason. A healthy partnership between emotion and reason is a conscious choice.

We need a balance between our emotions and reason before they work together to bring the searchlight of happiness. We do not grow old by merely living a number of years. We grow old by failing to grow from valley times. Being forever youthful is a temper to will to effort. Youth is a quality in our imaginations, our energy, and a freshness that comes from not being trapped by life's negatives.

Age brings wrinkled skin, but giving up being filled with enthusiasm wrinkles our souls.

We have a purpose, each of us. We can blame our unhappiness on someone else. We can lose our zip on life being unfair. We justify our rage because we had a slow start, our parents were bums, our outward looks are disgusting, our health is poor, our friends are louses, or our children are in trouble.

Some of us don't enjoy what we do for our livelihoods. However, these same people resign themselves to put up with their miserable jobs as a means to buy things that they thing might bring some happiness. Examine your video of your mind again. That tape reveals that you would rather work at something you hate, because you can make more money than you could doing something you love, but get paid less. Henry David

Thoreau was thinking this as he wrote, "Most men lead lives of quiet desperation." If you love your work and make an honest living helping others, you are building a wealth of joy.

Choose to be happy with who you are, and with what you have. As you discover your life's purpose and experience happiness and joy as by-products, use some simple suggestions.

1. Recognize that inner nudging. Does your present job or work feel like a grind? If you have free time or holidays, do you find yourself doing something that you love to do? Those feelings of guilt, fear, anxiety, and guilt may be keys to knowing your purpose.

2. Bring your heart to your work. Do you have the passion, the courage to find a profession that you really enjoy? Having patience to find that job is valuable time well spent.

3. Listen to your inner voice. Be quiet so you can listen to your inner desires. Your purpose for living will come as a whisper that will remind you of what will bring you happiness.

4. Believe in possibilities. Have a joyful anticipation. Unearth the things that bring you joy.

5. Tune out the world starved for love. Listen to your inner voice even if it goes against advice from friends or family. Take a leap of faith. Trust your dreams.

6. Become willing to change. Don't be afraid of change that has resulted from your experiences.

7. Do what you dread doing. Be patience with yourself. Joy comes in the mourning. There is a fast road and a slow road. Choose your own path.

8. Take that first step. Like a baby, be willing to fall down, to step away from your comfort zone.

9. Have no regrets. Don't waste that time. You used the time to find the skills to use for your purpose.

Willa Cather, a Nebraska author, wrote, "That is happiness: to be dissolved into something complete and great." President Woodrow Wilson declared, "I would rather fail in a cause that will ultimately triumph than to triumph in a cause that will ultimately fail."

Our struggles may be many, but there is joy triumphing in the end. Within ourselves, we sense an instinct, a kind of chronic joy. Slow down and discover what kind of tasks you enjoy. Perhaps finding a hobby will yield your life purpose. Maybe you really like to work with children. Maybe you find you like to organize events or create block parties. Some of us get in a flow, a kind of timeless zone, when we do something we truly enjoy. That's it. Could your instinct reveal that you are pursuing something that you have a genuine talent for?

As you consider what kind of work or part of your life purpose to go for, think of those elective courses you enjoyed in school. Where do you enjoy volunteering? Perhaps there are certain books or magazines you just naturally want to read. Your spare time fun activities might be a clue. If money were no object, what sort of business would you start? Now how do these things you do sort of by instinct view as a career.

Opportunities are spontaneous like the emotion joy. They show up in unexpected places. Perhaps it never occurred to you that you could do something different. The foundational issue is our life purpose. That's where the joy is. Connecting with other people where you add to the wealth of joy in the world adds to your own happiness and those moments of *jouissance*. Listen to your joy instincts. They come from a very special place. Take the risk. Your door has been opened to know your life purpose.

Surround yourself with people who believe in and will help you achieve your goals. Have lunch with them. Those lovely people who are willing to help are the ones you value and desire on your side. Realistically, people are rude, crude, and indifference. Sometimes even we are that way. Those people will tell you that your life purpose is just too big for you, not executable, and just ludicrous to even consider. These negative people tell us our dreams just cannot be done. Don't listen to the negativity. Of course, as we reach goals, we must be careful not to take on too many at one time. Remember, our purpose takes time and energy. We are human beings not human doings.

We were designed to all function in the same way. We are more alike than we are different. Our most important organ is the brain. Our brains secrete chemicals corresponding to our negative or positive thinking. The efficiency of our brain can be increased by optimizing the chemistry of our brain's cranial fluid.

Few of us can explain our electrochemical nervous system. We can't even list the numerous chemicals that affect our behavior. Of course, we don't even know the chemical composition of gasoline. People in Nebraska know that corn can be used to make gasoline. We just turn the key in the ignition, step on the pedal, and the car runs. We know that if we just put water in the gas tank, it won't run. We do not have to get a degree in chemistry to drive the car. Nor do you have to get a doctorate in neurobiochemistry to know what you need to know about transmitters like serotonin.

We know that higher levels of serotonin in our blood will

enable us to better performance and more positive thinking. Positive emotions cause chemical changes that help heal the body.

Mind, body, and spirit are connected. Negative thought instincts cause our brains to secrete chemicals that immediately impair our work performance. This awareness can enable us to be more objective. We can tune into the joy instinct. Just like a fine-tuned automobile engine designed to run on super high-octane gasoline will sputter if we put regular gasoline inside the gas tank.

This happens when we let the negative emotional instincts have power over us. We put low octane chemicals into our brains, causing our think and do tanks to suffer. When we act on our joy instinct, our brains secrete super high-octane chemicals. Our brains receive input through the five senses. Whenever we smell, taste, see, hear, or feel anything in our environment, the sense stimuli enters our nervous system as an electrical impulse through a nerve cell called a neuron. After that electrical message reaches the end of the neuron called a synapse, then the electrical impulse or message converts into a chemical that is a neuron transmitter. The chemical message is changed back into an electrical message or impulse when it reaches the next neuron. It is complicated. This process repeats itself until the message reaches the brain and we act on it.

When we are positive and operate on the joy instinct, our brain functions with the correct chemicals, or in our metaphor, on the high octane chemicals. We feel great and we excel. We become aware of our excellence as human beings. And we want to share it with others. We have "good chemistry" with other human beings that we enjoy being with. We also have "bad chemistry" with others. Some people may experience it as intuition.

Increasing Our Joy and Life's Purpose

We can increase our natural ability to know happiness and times of joy by adjusting the chemistry in our brains. That chemistry is made up of cranial fluid. And that fluid is affected by our thoughts. It is also affected by our physiology, our environment, our restfulness, our exercise, and our diet.

Positive or negative thinking cause our brains to secrete chemicals. Increased awareness of the damage done by negative thoughts can be done as we slow down and think about the facts of our life experiences. The facts take on emotions. Our imagination and perception of those facts have a profound influence on brain chemistry.

Chemicals include everything we eat, everything we drink. We are human beings. We naturally need proper amounts of fat, carbohydrates, and protein. Eating well is better advice than don't eat or diet. Diets never work. Just eat well in moderation. We don't have to become neurotics about our food.

Go to the Gymnasium If You Have To

Humans in their early days of existence used to run, jump, hunt, and lift weights. Our bodies are designed to move the muscles. Physical exertion removes toxins and helps us tap into positive emotional instincts by secreting those beneficial chemicals. For depression, nothing works as well as exercise. Some people get addicted to exercise. If you can't work in the lawn or garden, walk in your neighborhood, and move all your muscles, go to the gymnasium.

Create an Atmosphere for Joy

Creating an atmosphere for joy should be our life's mission. When we think about atmosphere, most of us think about the air we breathe or our physical surroundings. It also means the people around you at home, or in school, or in your church or community group.

We need to associate with positive people. If we find nothing in the above that stimulates happiness and joy, we can stay with ourselves. Of course, we are with negative people when we are trying to help them. Our happiness attitude could affect their lives. Our attitudes are as contagious as the common cold or even the flu. Mood infection strikes immediately.

It's not easy to remain positive with negative people. We can be influenced by their negative attitudes.

When we are "in a joy," we look positive and confident. We stand straight with our chests out. We have a smile on our faces. Imagine if your child told you that they were giving you a new grandson. Wouldn't we just feel like the wealthiest person in the world? Filled with joy, we would carry ourselves well. And we would share the joy within everyone we ran into.

Imagine how you would feel if you child called to say that the baby died or that the baby was deformed. Most of us would be depressed. Our eyes would be down. Our shoulders would slump. How we carry our bodies reflects our feelings. We can improve our brain chemistry by changes our physiology. Even something simple as standing tall, sticking the chest out, or talking some slow deep breaths can improve our chemistry. Lift your head and smile. Do it right now. For us to create an atmosphere for joy, we must work consciously on increasing the chemistry of our cranial fluid so we can perform at more efficient and joyful levels.

Your own life story with its hills and valleys is more important than anybody else's experiences. So you take a few minutes or longer to think about or write down your own personal experiences and stories of how positive or negative emotional instincts affected your happiness.

Confucius said, "Choose a job that you really love and you will never have to work a day in your life." Help other people find joy and you'll find some for yourself.

We may never know where our talents will lead. What our life purpose enables us to do to help others depends on our attitude. As we do what we have power to do, the blessings will come back to us, a hundred times over again.

An old Chinese proverb says, "If you want to be happy for an hour, take a nap. If you want to be happy for a day, go fishing. If you want to be happy for a week, take a vacation. If you want to be happy for a month, get married. If you want to be happy for a year, inherit a fortune. If you want to be happy for the rest of your life, help other people."

Creating an Atmosphere Where Joy and Miracles Happen

A woman from Weeping Water, Nebraska, told me about the Egyptians who lived in Bible times.

Before they died, they dealt with some serious questions before departing to the afterlife. One question was: "Did you find joy?" The second one: "Did you bring joy?"

Finding you for yourself, your family, church, and community means to decide to create an atmosphere for life that focuses on gratefulness for what you have. You can create this attitude by refusing to allow yourself to think in terms of scarcity, that is, there not being enough in this world for everybody.

We learn that joy is possible when life was going as we thought it should go. So we develop a habit of abandoning a joy-driven thought in favor of sadness when life is not as we thought it should be. We were then encouraged to believe that sorrow was natural. We think people suffer and suffer and suffer, and then they die. But that is not clear thinking. It is not the truth. In Genesis, God called everything that was created as "very good"—that means "full of joy, passionate joy, *jouissance*."

Creating this atmosphere or place where joy and miracles happen is to bring the spirit or energy of God to everything we encounter by changing or renewing our minds.

Time passes quickly when we are "in a joy." That same time just creeps along slowing in a grief or depression.

When we are inspired and involved joyfully in a work or project, time appears to fly. Time's appearance as tempus fugit or even if time is perceives as slow moving is perceived because time is an illusion. We invented time to carve up the oneness that is not divisible.

Time cannot exist when all is now.

Chronic joy melts time into oneness of spirit and time disappears. So living with a mission, a vision brings us into how God must view time.

Fulfilling our vision is being in a joyous present where time cannot exist.

Slow time appears when we are sad. Children express sadness on slow, long, boring trips. The deeper we move into grief, sorrow, melancholy, depression, and sadness the slower time appears to move. It's the same perception of time viewed from positive and negative thinking. Moments of grief are interminable. The times for death, divorce, loss of job, health, love causes us to look at the clock and find it impossible to believe that only fifteen minutes have passed.

Passionate joy speeds up the time illusion while depression and sad times slow it down. Joy-time is God-time. Eternal joy-time. Notice how much we are drawn to people with a positive, joyous outlook! We become filled with the joy instinct and become people who radiate love and the positive joyous energy that we can call none other than our *jouissance*.

Set Your Soul on Fire

Nothing in life that's worth using our life purpose for is easy. Helping others involves risk. Draw from your inner reservoir of strength and courage and go for it. You are the most power person on earth when your soul is on fire. Use your gifts to fire up your passion with your individual joy instinct. You will make a huge difference in the lives of people all around you. Your gifts will never be destroyed by your struggles and pain. No illness can defeat your spirit. Passionate joy drives out persistent depression.

By getting in touch with our joy instincts, we send powerful messages about the human spirit to every person in our circle. We may become the only person that our neighbor or friend knows who is having valley days. And we represent each one of us. A little church in Nebraska had a banner in front of the pulpit. It read, "To the world you might be just one person, but to one person, you might be the world."

Before we can send joy where there is sadness, we must first work on our personal life patterns. We must resolve to live with our joy instinct. This kind of life is created within an atmosphere where we feel and know purpose and mission as frequently as possible.

Moving to doing vision or mission is like bathing yourself in joy. Some people spend 50 years around people with developed joy instincts, but never catch it for themselves. Joy people think joy thoughts. They are not concerned with how they are being perceived by others. They don't so much pursue happiness and joy as they bring happiness and joy.

Jouissance can be found in the absence of striving for it, and instead realizing that joy is within us. It will not be realized by anything or anyone external to us. Purpose comes as we suspend our ego, knowing that we are eternally connected to God, and surrendering our little minds to the big mind. Joy comes by allowing the joy instinct to guide our lives. Then we will not have to ask what our purpose is or how to find it.

We feel purposeful in everything we do. We share joy with all that we encounter. We will bring joy to a world starving for love because we are in harmony rather than in conflict with God. Our spirit of passionate joy will link up with God's passions.

We will discover our own joy while we are giving it away.

PRACTICAL APPLICATION

We get ourselves into a corner when we believe we can avoid pain and problems if we only do it right—eat right, think right, image right, do spiritually right. Even with the best planning and organizing, we may have tough times or get sick. Even the "good" changes bring feelings of loss. The spiritual journey is not about getting rid of life's difficulties, it's about dancing with them.

Write in your personal journal a reaction to the thought by Margaret Lee Runbeck, "Happiness is not a station you arrive at, but a manner of traveling."

Now in light of CHAPTER 1, write down some of your "joy" stops on your journey.

Write song lyrics about it.

Perhaps you have a poem to share. Enjoy.

II

JOY AND OUR
HUMAN CONDITION

If you were all alone in the universe with no one to talk to, no one with which to share the beauty of the stars, to laugh with, to touch, what would be your purpose in life? We must discover the joy of each other, the joy of challenge, the joy of growth.

— Mitsugi Saotome

E MOTION IS ROOTED IN PERSONAL human experience. Two people can experience the same event and yet feel different emotions. A person standing at the edge of a river, who had earlier enjoyed the plunge, might feel joy at the daring dive. Another person, new to diving into that river, feels fear.

SEARCHING FOR INTERNAL AND EXTERNAL JOY RESPONSES

Why do we do the things we do? What causes us to think as we do? Most of us do what we do to make ourselves happy or to keep ourselves from becoming unhappy. That's why it is important to understand the human condition. View the videos in your mind. Different emotions reflected in your mind affect your view of the human condition. We do things because of what is on our videos of our personal human condition.

Human beings depend on people and things outside of

themselves for joy experiences. They depend on possessions to elicit a joy response. Some even resort to endless hours of television believing that one more show might give them something positive. Maybe watching sports or playing games will do it, we think. We take in every sort of external thing to make us happy or at least to mask our unhappiness. We are looking for happiness outside ourselves.

SEEKING JOY OUTSIDE OURSELVES

Advertising experts are well aware that we seek joy outside of ourselves. We give in to the instinct of buying what they are selling for us to feel good. Why do we do that?

We do it because we listen to the external voices that make us buy things, almost on automatic pilot. Depending on external factors for gaining joy wears off. So we keep looking outside ourselves for more possibilities. The more we obtain, the more we need to maintain our current contentment.

We have all heard the expression, "Money can't buy happiness." Now what is true about that? True and lasting happiness come from within. Joy is an internal response.

Reducing or eliminating our dependency on things outside ourselves to create joy and happiness, depends on structuring life so we find positive things inside. Nobody or no thing can take an experience of internal joy away from us.

Internal joy depends on our stopping selfish thinking about our human condition and focusing on other people. Our brain secretes positive chemicals corresponding to our positive emotions. When we reach out to build a wealth of joy in the world we are being generous with our time and resources. We show courage because we are not afraid of losing out while we are helping someone else instead on dwelling on ourselves.

And, of course, as a wonderful side benefit, our positive emotions elevate our chemistry, allowing our natural abilities to increase as well as our health. By helping others in our circles of influence, we raise our good chemical makeup and we do life at higher levels. Helping others gives internal joy. Choose a career and find a life purpose that gives you enjoyment, where you help others in the world while you earn your living.

We might not build material wealth this way, but we'll build a wealth of joy.

Also, the more positive we become, the less stress we will experience in our lives. Internal joys put a smile on the faces of those who know it and those who know the person behind the natural smile. The world will see it in your eyes.

EMOTION AS A COGNITIVE PHENOMENON

Emotions are a cognitive phenomenon. This cognitive aspect of feelings can be observed by examining how a person describes an emotional experience. During some terrifying ordeal, one person would report feeling no fear. Fear comes into the picture afterwards, when the thought about what happened is processed.

One mental health practitioner reported doing "cognitive therapy" and "not dealing with the feelings side of persons undergoing therapy." To do one is to do both. A person only laughs when they understand a joke, that is, when they get it. Emotions are descriptions of a state of the mind. Our minds have a method of communicating significant knowledge. Without emotions, our minds would have no method of informing other minds of the value of a life experience.

Our emotions take over the mind. They always have a physical component. So they cannot be ignored. Emotions connect us to each other and to the world as they help us understand profoundly what is going on.

Joy is the least discussed human emotion. From the results of creating a dynamic model of joy, we know that joy is the most important emotion. Joy communicates to ourselves and to others that we experience joy, and we are alive. The physical components of a joy experience, the flushed face, sensations of bodily well-being and alertness, easy laughter, ensure that in joy, the understanding of aliveness cannot be missed.

Jouissance is the emotion of aliveness, the fire of life. During an experience of creativity, joy is the ultimate expression of human potential. It can be experienced by humans relating to nature. It is felt by feelings produced by love. Joy is an emotion that communicates a sense of involvement with other people with a positive human event.

Starving for love, people cannot build much joy. And with an absence of joy, and through fear or anger, guilt and anxiety, human beings can understand that they are not free.

Joy is an existential emotion. Joy shares a base in a particular style of being in the world with a "will to openness" as opposed to a "will to power" as found in anger. Joy is rarely studied in psychology. The little past research on joy has led to a few discoveries. Most of us use the terms "joy" and "happiness" interchangeably. Joy is a positive emotion experienced in a particular time. Happiness involves an attitude toward all of life which includes all our human emotions.

These studies suggest that joy emerges when a person subjectively evaluates the life context to be familiar and safe. Another characteristic of joy is when our given task requires little effort. Reasonable progress to a goal is reasonable to assume.

Further, joy has been found to be an intrinsic component of peak experiences. It has been associated with playfulness. In play the action is open and non-specific. Further, joy functions to affirm the meaningfulness of life. This delight time discloses a certain experience of mattering and fortunateness with the characteristic of a gift. We are thankful for the gift.

Asking people about their individual joy experiences is fun whether in a group or during a community function. To ground people in a concrete remembrance of a time of joy, we can use a therapy technique called the Imagery in Movement Method. This method involves using drawing skills or sketches, gestures, and role playing to induce an existential felt emotional memory. The participants will then record their joy experience in a written narrative. The resultant reports are fun and nobody minds sharing their joy.

In a group therapy or psychology of joy group, the participants' stories are concrete with an abundant amount of experiential details.

MEMORIES OF TIMES OF JOY

Memories of the birth of a child, a special surprise given at a special time, a wedding, waking up alive from a dangerous operation were frequent themes.

During a winter retreat, a man described his first memory of a Christmas morning. He recalled in gesture and in words the sense of wonder and then his utter exhilaration he felt as he walked down the stairs in his home with his sister and brother to be aware of the Christmas tree with presents all around it. His descriptions were ripe with metaphor. His jouissance was felt as an elation geyser shooting up his torso and up into his head like the sparkling tinsel dangling from the limbs of the tree.

Another person, a little girl who had learned to ride horses, described the exuberance of bounding across the finish line when her horse won her first race. Her words included the joy as s world that arced toward a baby-spanked sky, expansive with the fullness of possibility.

Still another person shared a blissful moment playing with her cousins in a meadow surrounded by mountains. As she lost herself in a dance with them, she felt the world as powerful, cradling her softly as a mother embraces a child.

We are always touched by the sharing of a joy. Sometimes we weep as a man shared that his surgeon related he might not make it through the surgery. He risked it, and in tears felt his joy moment as he awakened, smiling warmly at his family.

Nothing is more helpful to anyone's fulfillment as being enabled to remember a long forgotten yet nourishing moment of life.

ANALYZING JOY EXPERIENCES

Using an empirical-phenomenological method for analysis and a report from four conferences in Oxford, England, the participants identified sixteen themes of the reported joy experiences. The world in which joy emerges was experienced in a context that was powerful yet benevolent. The joyful reporter felt centered with a profound sense of being in the present moment. Each felt open to any possible experience. And they were not pursuing a particular outcome. Their engagement with the world was not instrumental. So joy spontaneously happened. Their joys were all spontaneous. They felt the freedom just to be in a sense of highness, a highlight of life kind of event. The stories always showed connection to others, a deep interpersonal connectedness. They were affirmed and nurtured by the powerful and benevolent world that graced their life. Each walked away from sharing their joy as a renewed sense of gratitude for living. In this appreciation for the simple and pure fact that each of us is valued, joy is an ontological emotion. That is, joy reveals the meaning of our being.

Other values perceived were perfection, completion, justice, wholeness, richness, aliveness, goodness, uniqueness, effortlessness, playfulness, wholeness, beauty, simplicity, and self-sufficiency. Being as revealed in a joy experience is not understood as a mere extension of our own wants and needs. Joy comes in an all-inclusive full circle, not just as something that is ours alone. It shows a good world, not an evil one. A joy-filled person knows an altered sense of time and space described as "infinite" or "eternal." Participants said they felt childlike, transported back to a more free and playful time.

SIMPLE MODELS FOR DESCRIBING JOY

We begin with the words participants used in sharing joy. Words such as amusement, bliss, cheerfulness, contentment, delight, elation, enjoyment, enthrallment, enthusiasm, euphoria, excitement, exhilaration, gaiety, gladness, hope, jolliness, joviality, jubilation, optimism, pleasure, pride, rapture, relief, satisfaction, zest, and zeal were included. Use some of these words to describe a joy experience of your own.

PROMPTING EVENTS FOR FEELING JOY

What were the life happenings that prompted joy? Highlighted themes included: Being successful at doing a task; being with or in connection with a person loved; belonging to people who accept us as we are; receiving love or affection; doing things that create or bring to mind pleasurable sensations; achieving a desired outcome; getting what you need or want; receiving respect or praise; receiving a surprise; transitions turning out better than we could ever expect; reality exceeding expectations; and gaining recognition or surprising gifts.

Interpretation of these prompting events came just as they were without adding anything to embellish them.

EXPERIENCING JOY

Experiencing joys included feeling excited, hyper, energetic, active, laughing, smiling, flushing of the face, leaping or jumping, raising the hands, or giving a big hug to any person within your space. We might talk excessively, use an enthusiastic or excited voice, say positive things, and share the feeling with a bouncy face.

Afterwards, joy-filled people do nice things for other people, expect to repeat a joy time, remember other times when they were in a joy, see the bright side, and become courteous and friendly. Joy makes us aware of the grace we can know in our human condition. Joy is truly a gift, an emotion of grace that we can never create by ourselves not matter where we are or who we are. Human beings feel that they are debtors and creditors to each other. We feel owing or being owed to with our circles of other people. We move through life wondering how people and life will respond to us.

Volunteering and helping others confirms that we still

have something good to offer. Enabling other people who have been wounded looks like a huge undertaking. Taking our minds off of ourselves and placing them selflessly on others will be to our souls as water is to the thirsty. Somebody is always saying, "There's always somebody worse off than you." We can fully understand that truth when we reach out and help someone else. You will never feel worse by volunteering. Assisting others who have experienced the same sort of valleys and bad days as we have gives us a double skill. Helping those with a similar human condition will enable us to know that we are not the only person who has a serious problem. And as we continue to help, it only makes us feel better. Mark Twain said, "The best way to cheer ourselves up is to try to cheer someone else up."

JOY AS AN UNCOMMON GRACE

If joy were depicted as a color, it would be one of the primary hues, but it would require a complicated formula to get it mixed at a Sherwin–Williams store. What are the layers or the ingredients that enables us to experience joy?

There once was a man who drank too much. He was young, strong, and in the prime of his life. He had a huge salary and all the material comforts one could imagine. There was no history of alcoholism in his family. But something was bothering him about his condition.

When asked why he drank so much, he finally admitted, "Because I am afraid of death." Joy is an uncommon grace. It is our final destiny.

We are given strength and power beyond our own capacity to deal with the human condition. Granted in some of our human experiences, the Higher Power might have appeared paltry at the time because we really wanted a dramatic rescue. That power would have been more detectable as we look back on our human condition, but it was power, nonetheless.

Joy is magnetic and contagious. Joyful people can't contain it. Joy never travels incognito, never puts on sunglasses and a scarf. Joy is there to bless and to invite others to experience it for themselves. Milton Erickson said, "Life will bring you pain all by itself. Your responsibility is to create joy."

POWER MADE PERFECT IN WEAKNESS

What does it mean to have courage in the midst of our pain, suffering, and death? People write many books idolizing strength in adversity. Courage has another side. Most of us are not forced to think about it. It is revealed when our vulnerability is demonstrated and our own strength is exhausted.

The apostle Paul wrote that God's power is made perfect in our weakness. We stigmatize weakness. We see no value in suffering. Suffering is not the worst of our human condition. It is worst to do evil rather than to suffer from it. We need not fear weakness. Suffering can be our crucible of transformation, an opportunity for new visions, deeper joys.

Of course, we don't glorify suffering for its own sake. Suffering isn't good. It is not an end in itself. The courageous suffering in our human condition is not endurance of pointless pain in a meaningless world. The suffering we bear is often the result of trying to give to love starved people in a world that has missed the mark. Some of us suffer in trying to help our own family. What can we do? We feel powerless in trying to understand our own family environment.

ENDURING OUR FAMILY ENVIRONMENT

Children suffer in silence as they endure their family environment. We suffer from guilt, fear, and anger. Anxiety fills the room when joyless family members come together. Anxiety can stuff our joy. It is a fear of the unknown. This feeling is worse than an ordinary fear of some specific thing. Anxiety leaves you feeling powerless and vulnerable. We will do anything to avoid it. So we learn to react in certain ways in order to avoid feeling anxious. Many of us become depressed. We are paranoid, wondering how people, especially authorities and bosses, will react to us. That person who has been formally or informally in control of us has the power to curb your joy and make you feel anxiety.

If as a child, we broke a written or unwritten, spoken or unspoken rule, parents might have used physical punishment. Some use the threat of withdrawing love. This plays on our fear of abandonment that everyone experienced when growing up. As an adult, we fear losing a job, perhaps for ministers the fear is receiving no appointment, for professional athlete the fear is being tossed off the team. Even the threat of abandonment triggers anxiety, so we try to change or conform to avoid the anxious pain.

A child is having fun playing on the park's play equipment. Her mom comes over and says that it is time for them to leave. The child says "no." She's having fun. Mom could just pick her up and put her in her car seat. But often moms will use psychology. She just walks away and says, "Stay here and enjoy the park. I'm going home." After mom gets near the car, she runs toward her mother.

Abandonment is a control method. It controls our personality. Because we needed mother as a child, and now we need our bosses so much, we suppress the parts of our personality that authorities find objectionable rather than to have to suffer the pain of anxiety. We believe we cannot make it on our own. So we best not do something they judge as wrong, for they are both judge and jury. We learn that it is dangerous to be ourselves. If we don't become anxious, then those trying to control us get anxious. We have to learn how to be sensitive to other people's anxiety. One mother said to her child, "You've had your joy. Now let's get home right now." Sometimes we are the trigger of their anxiety.

We may eat the best food, exercise our bodies regularly, but still suffer from cancer. We can hold a perfectly clean driving record, but still end up suffering in the hospital after being in an accident with a drunk driver.

Enduring suffering is difficult for us. We are so afraid of it. But be assured that joy will have the last word. We enjoy eternal life because our bodies are joined to spirit or soul. With our joy instinct we have the ability to understand truths that are beyond us. We know our spirit or soul receives a glimpse of life's working together to teach us in every thing we experience.

ALL THINGS WORKING TOGETHER FOR GOOD

When life is going well after the valleys of pain and suffering have been experienced, we somehow accept it all as good. That's what we call happiness. We can look back to all that we have suffered and we realize that our souls really are tough. Our souls are made for endurance. We reflect upon all the misery and uncertainty, when we didn't think we could last another day or even another hour. We look forward to the time of relief.

We think that we will then be content, satisfied, and perhaps even lucky. But that's not how it is with us. We experience a kind of regret, a strange sadness, that we now know a loss instead of a gain.

We begin to realize that those valley times had a vividness of a reality far more intense than our easier present. And sometimes an old song or a word or a movie brings it all back. Of course it was grim and painful, and we paid dearly for it. But if we had not gone through it, we would not be who we are now. Even though we are glad it's over and "the feeling's gone and we can't get it back again," somehow we needed that low time.

We bear the valley times—the low times—through chronic joy. We have within us an instinct for negative emotional response or to a joy response. In the next chapter we'll unearth your joy instinct.

PRACTICAL APPLICATION

Write a note on "What is Joy?"

Reflect on your joy as not being "mind-blowing," but a quiet, peaceful, simple pleasure.

Write a list on words that you associate with joy. Start with gladness, peacefulness, delight, and exuberance. Or if you are fluent in another language, write in those words.

Use other words that say "joy" to you.

Make a sculpture or paint a picture to help you take in and understand the human feeling of joy.

III

CHRONIC JOY

Sometimes your joy is the source of your smile, but sometimes your smile can be the source of your joy.

— Thich Nhat Hanh

MOMENTS OF *JOUISSANCE*, EXCESSIVE RADICAL chronic joy, rarely come with an instant, intense revelation that Sartre understood as "a burst of realization."

Our "burst of realization" comes as we decide that tomorrow is today. Most children are born with a chronic joy. Children up to preschool time laugh up to 400 times each day. Adults average about seven times per day. Research has shown a connection between joy and laughter. Laughter strengthens our immune system. Laughter helps us breathe better. It slows aging. It enables us to sing the sad songs of life.

TAP INTO YOUR CHRONIC JOY INSTINCT

Goethe said, "Whatever you can do, or dream you can, begin it. Boldness has genius, power, and magic in it." As our dreams pass through the sieve of life, what comes out is a watered-down version of what we discover as our life purpose. If we allow ourselves the freedom of doing away with the sieve of life, our chronic joy instinct will enable us to live our dreams every moment, not just once a day, or each month, or even each year. How can we tap into our joy instinct? What is chronic joy? Each of us can permit chronic joy to influence us more than our guilt, fear, anxiety, or anger instincts.

Chronic joy means if your schedule could be revised erasing the weekly meetings, grocery store trips, television, or time-consuming but necessary chores, what would you choose to do? Passionate joy comes in a schedule given over to your passion.

Would you shoot some basketball or do a round of golf, be with your life partner or your children or just relax and do nothing? Remember you're free and spontaneous with your chronic joy instinct. Envision one hundred things you'd really enjoy doing. Chronic joy is living your life with no filters. Joy helped us to not be worried about money, self-esteem or relationship issues, or the joy-blockers. Now consider how you can help build a wealth of joy in the world starved for love.

Without the life filter to limit your vision, you can discover your personal purpose, you calling, the person you were created to become. Negative messages block many people from ever knowing or hearing clearly. We must give ourselves time to listen. No matter how lonely, afraid, or ill you are right now, there is a chronic joy instinct inside. Life built around your personal truth has no choice but to have happiness in the midst of any and all of life's burdens.

Some of us might answer life's essential questions early, even as children. Perhaps your life is filled with adversity. In some of our homes we reflected on our poverty, our family dysfunction, or our health limitations. Our chronic joy instinct enabled us to see beyond our outer environment. Joy can rule even with our valley times, our pain, suffering, and frustration. Restructure your human condition by first restructuring your negative thinking. A shift in focus will push us to work and dream within our limitations to fulfill our life purpose. What could each person do today to enable them to become the person they'd like to be? For some, the following exercise did not cause regret, but rather, it tapped into their chronic joy instincts.

AN EXERCISE OF LOOKING AT THE BIG PICTURE

In one of Dr. John Killinger's classes, a student created an authentic-looking obituary section of the *Nashville Tennessean*. All members of this class were in the story, which featured the lives of each person. A building had collapsed on the Vanderbilt campus, and we had all died amidst the rubble.

Perhaps the exercise appears morose, but there was value in asking, "How, specifically, do we want to be remembered during our days of living? What legacy will we leave behind?

Members of the class were in stunned silence. Some stories gave tangible evidence that they had made the world a richer place. Some sensed that outside their flaws and wounds from life, they had been kind, honest, persistent, and caring.

The class was challenged that if they did not care for their obituary, why not? They were challenged to take actions now that would reflect becoming the best they could be in the future despite their past.

WHAT WILL YOU BE WHEN YOU GROW UP?

Now slip back to the days of your childhood. Children appear to have a natural instinct for joy. Have you noticed? Try to recall your thoughts at that time. Before the world made you aware of your limitations, what was your thinking like? What dreams came as you spent hours walking the hilltops, playing in the creek, building castles in the sand? You spent hours dreaming, what will I be when I grow up?

Some people used their joy instinct and became exactly what they dreamed. Think about people who played doctor or nurse and today those roles are their life vocation. These people always had a deep belief in themselves. They had an anticipation to joy, not a fearful anticipation.

You might be in one of your valley times. Try to visualize your next hilltop time. Tap into your natural joy instinct. Make a video of what you want to be. Take a mind photo to see a mental picture based on what instinctively is right for you. Don't dwell on what's not possible. Tell your life partner, one of your children, or a mentor about your personal picture. Write in your journal what you see. Read it often. Put it on your bathroom mirror, your computer monitor, or like your parents did when you were a child, on the refrigerator.

TO FAIL TO PLAN IS TO PLAN TO FAIL

Writing out our life plan will give us a clear vision. Keep it in mind. The more time you spent making your plan clear, the better your joy instinct will check in. Break your plan into part acts. Make it realistic. Perhaps your plan will include where you will live, who will be in your circle of relationships, what will be your career. Now do the first part action.

As you determine your personal part acts to success, stick to them. Celebrate each part of your accomplishment. Doable small part acts works with your joy instinct. You are getting things done despite your feelings or the realties of your valley times. You can rejoice that you have planned to succeed. You did move your muscles, and your brain rejoiced with you.

When we are "in a joy," we radiate with a glow on our faces. Chronic joy enables us to feel better and to look better. We reveal a deeper understanding and joy's exultation helps us stand proudly despite your illness or pain.

Few individuals are born with superlative gifts for art, music, mathematics, science, or leadership. Most of us are just average. Every person is born with the gift of living and the capacity for joy. Joy is a natural, normal emotion.

Each day passes too quickly. As we age, time flies faster and faster. The metaphor of a roll of toilet paper can capture this experience. When we are young, the roll looks like there is plenty left, so we use it without much awareness of how much is left. As we age, the roll appears smaller and smaller, quickly moving to the end. Building a wealth of joy means each day passes quickly but without regret, because tomorrow beckons even more invitingly. We just do the best we can, squeezing the most out of each day's living, being aware of chronic joy every minute.

There is no assurance that we can experience joy just by wanting it. We can be certain that we'll miss much of the readily available wealth of joy if we close our eyes to the possibility or turn away from it. We'll miss out if we have an outlook that says, "I just don't have the disposition or capacity for joy. I'm not the type."

That hopeless, self-defeating focus is nullified if we create an atmosphere that says, "The best times are ahead of us and we'll create the best possibilities for joy."

Concentrating on unhappiness is as obtuse and wasteful as throwing away a whole apple because a small part of it is rotten. Instead we can enjoy the rest, which is sweet and delicious. Norman Cousins decided to live in chronic joy as he was dying of cancer. He wrote, "The most costly disease in America is not cancer or coronaries. The most costly disease is boredom, costly for both the individual and society." G. K. Chesterton suffered long periods of deep depression. He emerged from the abyss with a strong conviction that "the fact of existence is in itself wonderful."

First we must believe that joy is not scarce. Believe that we are all entitled to be "in a joy" as much as the next person. We must develop a sense of chronic joy. We can endure and emerge from tragedies that hit us—loss of a loved one, a severe illness, or loss of material possessions, or a job. We will manage to go on without falling apart. Joy will come in the mourning.

EXPANDING OUR CAPACITIES FOR JOY

Our purpose is to reveal the joy in living to the fullest. Sharing the wealth of joy in this world means to open ourselves wider, to feel more of all human emotions, to savor every possible moment, every smallest loving day to the utmost of our abilities and capacities. We will come to realize that our attainments of every kind have and never will reach their fullest possible extent. Always we can expand to discover more, feel more, and enjoy more in our years given as a gift to all of us.

There is a wealth of joy, enough for everybody. We can step up the zest that we draw from the moments of our days. We can add to the videos of being in our joys. We can store these moments of *jouissance* in our minds to bring out during any down times. We will cherish and remember our joys feeding our ever-growing consciousness. Joy comes to us in ever-happening fragments every day if we keep ourselves open for opportunities and seek them watchfully. Inevitably we will find them, and hold them in our lasting remembrance as the gems of our days.

LONELY PEOPLE

As we build a wealth of joy for love-starved people we must do something about the loneliness in which many of them live. Loneliness prevents people from discovering joy. Without a passion to relate there can be no joy.

To change this state calls for much more than activity or goodwill by a few individuals, essential as that is. For loneliness and the deprivation of joy that it entails can become a habit that is not easily broken. People can reach a sad state of addiction to their loneliness. These people do not wish their adjustment to loneliness to be disturbed.

Those who wish to help heal people of this social evil, need, therefore, the guidance of science, psychology, social workers, and those in the helping professions, if we are to share the wealth of joy with the lonely.

We need to devise a comprehensive and informed strategy both to bring people out of their present loneliness and also to see that future generations do not fall into it.

Don't expect support from politicians. Sharing wealth of anything, much less joy, might be as little vote catching as the legislation for civil rights. Lonely people need an amelioration of their condition. This is not beyond the combined wit of humankind to provide it. Simone Weil said, "Sin is nothing else but the failure to recognize human wretchedness." Loneliness makes far more human beings much more wretched than the hardest of hard pornography or any other joy stealers. Joy stealers are life experiences that create a climate for negative experiences that are barriers to joy. Keep reading. We are on to something and we will go for it.

STRENGTHENING OUR INDIVIDUALITY

Striving for chronic joy does not mean becoming like everybody else. Experiencing this human emotion, joy, is an individual's part of the wealth of love. We'll discover as we absorb and think through conclusions for ourselves that we, as individuals, will build and strengthen our individuality.

Joy gives us a more invigorating and sustaining sense of self. We begin to believe in ourselves as we take in the joy. We store up even more wealth of joy as we share it with others. We get along better with ourselves and with others.

A cartoon in *The New Yorker* showed a saleswoman inside a greeting card store. She was working herself up, going berserk. She was screaming, "Greetings out there, all you happy people. Happy birthday! Happy anniversary! Happy graduation! Happy job promotion! Happy, happy, happy everything!" At least she learned that greeting cards can't create joy. Words have little relationship to the wealth of joy we are seeking.

Joy does not mean constant cheerfulness. Knowing moments of joy is not so much setting a destination as practicing the ways and means of getting there. Creating an atmosphere for joy builds in us an optimistic viewpoint. It does not help to say that things will get better if we hope and just wait long enough." Instead we must move our muscles to try consciously and determinedly to exert our energy toward making life better for everyone.

Explaining her individual concept, a woman said, "Peace

is that experience in which fear is unknown. But joy is a positive experience. In a joy experience something goes out from oneself to the universe, a warm, possessive effluence of love. There might be peace without joy, and there could be joy without peace, but the two combined create happiness."

We have our own simple or complicated definitions of the joy experience. Some individuals were asked in a research survey to define joy. Some say something like, "Joy is feeling good, depending on what makes people feel good." Just trying to define it is a step toward acquiring or knowing it.

Arthur Rubinstein, a gifted pianist, said at age 85, "We are given a short life. What we know is what our sense tells us— flowers, love, poetry, music. People think money, success, power are necessary. No! It's so absurdly stupid. I need only one flower in that corner there to have joy."

What do we need?

Chronic joy means squeezing every possible bit of joy out of every hour, every day, every moment. It means being aware of and uplifted by every scrap of joy that comes our way, or that we can share with each other every day.

A thoughtful mother refused to give a candy bar to her seven-year-old son. "Mom, you won't let me have any joy in life," the boy said.

The mother replied, "Ethan, soon you'll learn that joy is not found in eating a candy bar."

Joy is not what self-serving advertisers have proclaimed: "Joy is a $100 mattress." "Joy is a new brand of perfume." "Joy is a sexy, powerful car." "Joy is having a credit card with no limits on it." "Joy is a cell phone for a ten year old."

If we think that joy is something as inconsequential as a candy bar or some material thing, then we are underrating joy and ourselves. Those fleeting titillations are what a wealth of joy is not. The human emotion joy is not characterized by good fortune or luck or prosperity, pleasure, or satisfaction.

Joy becomes part of each individual's life experience not only by echoing and repeating the word, but by what we do, how we live, by our actions toward others, our interchanges with everyone we meet, and the awareness of the resultant deep-rooted radical joy within ourselves. Once joy experiences have been saved in the videos of our minds, *jouissance* is part of each of us lifting and sustaining us through good and bad times to a richer, more fulfilling life. It is beyond most people's understanding and beyond what most people will allow themselves.

EXCESSIVE JOY

Living daily with an awareness of joy brings with it moments of sheer exhilaration, excessive joy. They add up to that intoxicating state in which the whole person is centered on and in the sensation of having just been born, having just been set free, having been conceived for this freedom, this feeling.

Experiencing conscious joy gives us a repeated sense of a rebirth, that uplifting feeling of being a really new person, free, soaring in spirits, especially and wonderfully alive. This feeling of almost bursting with quiet *jouissance*, an exhilaration that all of us have experienced during our lifetimes.

We will savor this least discussed emotion more often in the future, and in a more fulfilling, deeper, lasting way, because we can become more conscious and appreciating the sensation. We cannot create a joy, but we can do more to create an atmosphere in our living that can enable us to know joy more often. Nikos Kazantzakis said, "We have our brushes. We have our colors. We can paint paradise and enjoy it." George Witkin put it another way, "Cultivate more joy by arranging your life so that more joy will be likely to be there."

If we were to live in a joy emotion forever, it could never be complete. Staying in joy forever would not create wealth. Just as the fairy tale about the old king who got tired of having everything he touched turn into gold, joy would no longer be our wealth, but a burden. There is no living state completely free of problems or cares. A happy life contains all emotions. Joy is like a flashlight shining on one event, happening, or connection during our lives. Happiness is like a searchlight revealing fear, anxiety, anger, and guilt as well as times of joy. Our lives could never work if we were ever joyous and lilting with no down experiences. Nobody can promise us that and fulfill that kind of pledge.

Joy is a powerful emotion. One time of joy can dispel a thousand cares. Even if we could imagine living in a joy forever, it would not make life complete. Mark Twain said, "On with the dance, let joy be unconfined is my motto, whether there's a dance to dance or any joy to unconfined." Dancing with joy forever would keep life at one lofty level, no further ups and downs on our charts of life, no changes, and no variety. Perhaps this living in a joy forever would be possible and appropriate in some other world. In our world, we would miss the spice of intangible excitement, the stimulating expectancy of experiencing something more, something challenging to look forward to and to strive for each day.

Life as we know it today is a continuous learning process. Each experience, each up and down, every hill and valley we pass through is another step in this learning process. All problems will not be eliminated, but our positive, courageous, searching attitude of chronic joy can reduce and accommodate the number and especially the effect of heavy, unavoidable burdens. Joy does not lie in the mere fact of having what we desire. Some things are a want not a need. Richard Wagner said, "Joy is not in things, it is in us." Later in this book, we will look at a psychology of joy. Understanding a model of human joy will not lead us to ignore or to bypass the ills and evils that exist in this world and in dialing living. While we care about and fight for a better way of life for ourselves and for others, we realize that whatever struggles buffet us, we can function most effectively when we are imbued with the inner peace and joys of living. William Barclay said, "Joy has nothing to do with material things, or with a man's outward circumstances. A person living in the lap of luxury can be wretched, and a person in the depths of poverty can overflow with joy."

Having those videos or memories of joy experiences in our brains can help us to be equipped to cope with the trails and pressures of living. And by knowing joy times for ourselves, we are better able to help others to derive the most from each day for ourselves, our families, and all who come in contact with us.

Jouissance, or excessive joy, experiences are rare in life. To live a life of happiness, we know we'll be coping with all negative and positive times, hills and valleys. If any of us are "in a joy" right now, in a hill time, we will hit the valley soon, but a chart of our individual days of living from birth to this very hour will go up and down as we connect the dots from each year of times in the hills and in the valleys.

William Blake wrote, "He who kisses the joy as it flies, lives in eternity's sunrise." We begin with the conviction that life is good. By just trying, just showing up with a courageous attitude, joy will come. The eternal sunrise aspects of our joys will enable us to realize and understand that troubles do exist and they will recur, but so will the joys, so we can live each day exerting ourselves to climb out of our valleys and back upon the hills where we can see all of life and say, "I like it."

Charles Swindoll said, "I believe the most significant decision I make on a daily basis is my choice of attitude. Attitude is what keeps me going or cripples my progress." After the initial shock and suffering have been felt in our lives, we make a choice as to how we will react to the troubles in our lives.

We could have an attitude of rage or anger. In this attitude we blame other people. We use our energy to keep our anger until others have suffered for the pain that caused us. This attitude never works.

Some of us remember when we had record albums. We recall what happened when one of the records got scratched. The needle was not able to move forward. Instead it was stuck at one point, and the record kept repeating itself. How annoying that was!

When we choose an attitude of rage, it's as if our lives are like a scratched record that is struck in one painful place. We are like a broken record. So people in our circles get tired of our complaining and grumbling and leave us behind.

Another joy-killing attitude is chronic self-pity. When we respond to adversity in this attitude, we are cynical, grumpy, negative, and pessimistic. We complain about everything. We do not laugh. We withdraw into our shells. We quit on life.

Chronic joy is the best attitude. Happiness indicates things are going well. We might be prosperous, victorious, healthy, and in satisfying relationships. Unfortunately, some of us get unhappy when life is in the valleys. It is much like dew that appears in the morning, but is gone a few hours later.

Joy is a chronic, excessive attitude. It is with us even when things aren't going well. It is an attitude of contentment even amidst suffering and pain. Most of us would like to develop and keep an attitude of joy. A key to this chronic attitude is to give love away. Irish writer Anna Jameson said, "What we truly and earnestly aspire to be, that, in some sense, we are. The mere aspiration of changing our frame of mind, for the moment, will realize itself."

To change our attitude, we must pay attention to life's wake-up calls. We create problems for others and ourselves by the choices we have made. The only thing that keeps us from staying with a bad attitude are wake-up calls which are often dramatic events such as a heart attack that suddenly causes us to realize that we have not been taking care of our bodies.

A teenaged South African boy was asked by his father to drive them to the nearest city, which was about eighteen miles from home. He jumped at the chance to drive. Because they were going to town, his mother asked him to buy groceries. His father asked him to have the car serviced. His father told him to pick him up at five o'clock.

After getting the shopping done, the boy dropped off the car at the garage and then went to a local movie theater. He was so interested in the film that he forgot the time. Suddenly, he noticed it was now 5:30 p.m. By the time he picked up the car and met his father, it was six o'clock.

When asked why he was late, the young man was ashamed to say that he was late because he had gone to see the movie.

He said, "The car was not ready. I had to wait." His father had already called the garage. When the boy was caught in the lie, his father said, "There's something wrong in the way I brought you up that I didn't give you the confidence to tell me the truth. In order to figure out what I did wrong with you, I'm going to walk home and think about it."

Because it was dark and the road was unpaved, the boy drove slowly as he watched his dad take five hours to make the long walk, all because he was stupid enough to tell a lie. As a result of that wake-up call, he vowed that he would never lie again.

CHANGE IS A LIFELONG PROCESS

Change will be genuine if it's demonstrated over an extended period of time by the way that we live and how we respond when we have setbacks. We are reminded that change is a lifelong journey. A helpful question to ask ourselves is: "If we have changed, do the people who know us best, see that we are different?"

COURAGE TO BE DIFFERENT

Courage is essential if we are changed. Being different requires an art, the art of not antagonizing people unnecessarily. This takes courage. People really don't object to our being different nearly as much as they object to our attitudes of superiority.

We can be ourselves, even if it is different, but we do have to be tolerant of the people who are different from us. If we would just give each other the right to be our own personality types, we would be different enough.

Take a look at your personality, your life, and check the areas where you are letting a foolish fear of "what people might think" hold you down or keep you back. Go for it. Do some of those unorthodox things.

The fears of being different tend to get less and less when you see yourself in the light and take the honest look. At the bottom of such fear lies a preoccupation with self. Most everything in life is a triviality. We keep quirks of our personal truths alive by agonizing about them. This kind of self-awareness is a form of egotism. Most of the disapproval, rejection, and disappointments we encounter are imaginary. Paranoid, we see menace where there is none. If we run into resentment and ridicule, we belong to a long line of wonderful people.

CREATING JOY

We have the power to create an environment for joy. Thoreau said, "If one advances confidently in the direction of his dreams, and tries to live the life which he has imagined, he will meet with a success unexpected in common hours." Our decisions can be based on our chronic joy instinct. We need not let the negative videos composed of fear, guilt, anxiety, and pain control our efforts.

Giving in to the joy instincts and playing our joy experiences, always available in our mind videos, will be a part of the miraculous. Our improbable dreams are possible realities. We can accomplish things we have long ago put out of our reach.

Our efforts will duplicate every time we share them. Our stories will inspire others. And some those all around will respond to our glowing. The ripple effect kicks in. Next thing we know, good positive feelings are spreading like the Wave at a football game.

By creating joy in even the worst life conditions, we will build a wealth of joy. In spite of monumental obstacles, we are able to let our joy instincts help us create all sorts of joyful

things. People all over the planet are starving for our joy baskets
that can be created only by those who know what joy really is.

PRACTICAL APPLICATION

Consider some facts about "joy." Add to these or compose your own list.

1. We have the right to be joyful.

2. We have the potential for joy.

3. Joy comes from within ourselves. Knowing and liking yourself is a prerequisite to a full experience of joy.

4. Joy comes from simple pleasures without intense ecstatic or euphoric considerations.

5. Being in chronic joy does not mean you will never be sad or depressed.

6. Moments of joy come in the midst of difficult circumstances.

7. An unrealistic definition and psychological model of joy might prevent us from being open to everyday joy experiences.

8. Extrinsic and counterfeit experiences with food, drugs, things, or people cannot give joy.

9. Joy is a rare study for scientists and spiritual people. Few understand joy. Passionate joy can enable one to overcome dispassionate depression.

IV

PSYCHOLOGY OF JOY

Psychology and psychiatry offer help to the emotionally ill, but offer little direction for high-level emotional wellness, for how to be healthy and joyful each day.

—Paul Pearsall

W E RARELY EXPRESS JOY. We do not hear about it in school. Our mentors fail to bring it up. Even our spiritual directors miss describing those savoring moments missed by our patterned numbness to that thrill of being most alive. These moments of living in "eternity's sunrise" have been stored up in our minds on videotapes that are in our brains at this minute. How can we look up those videos of "the glorious life that is within us?"

Most of us are content to be average or normal. Moments of being in joy are startles or peak experiences. Reviewing our joy with ourselves and others enhances self-esteem, helps us cope with difficult times, and to expand our emotional domain.

Wounded by lack of awareness of joy, we become addicted to failure, to depression, to life out of synch. We continue to ride the rollercoaster of busyness and normality, rewarded by a world that rewards those who obey and to fit in.

Joy is a precious, yet rare human response. One reason our therapists fail to mention joy is that all of us never escape our overheated lifestyle that holds out impossible expectations. We become human doings not human beings. How many hospitals or mental hospitals discuss "joy" during the course of therapy? We discuss guilt. Almost every treatment center has an anger management class or group. Anxiety groups are at the top of the list of groups. And so is a discussion of fear included.

Normal or addictive behavior is easy, even positive addictions to running or dancing or support groups for everything that becomes a barrier to our joy is included in healing us.

BUILDING A MODEL OF JOY

How do we build a model for a psychology of joy? There has been a study or book about the psychology of most every human activity. Also, there are books on the joy of everything including the joy of sex, the joy of money, even the joy of old age.

First, joy is a human emotion. Human emotions include anger, anxiety, guilt, fear. Most any experience of life can be described with a model using these five emotions. Emotions might be described as human reflexes, response systems, and mental perceptions. In some treatment programs, emotions are downplayed or ignored. Those who use these approaches will tell us, "Don't tell me how you feel. Tell me how you function."

During the joy response, people and objects of value around us are perceived as good. Self-esteem is enhanced. Celebration happens and we are free to cry, to laugh out loud, to jump, to turn a cartwheel, to shout in natural unencumbered ways. Joy responses are spontaneous, immediate, and real. And whenever we experience joy, we just have to share it. We can easily describe five people who we think experience little joy. But to tell of five people who have chronic joy despite difficulties gives us a problem. People who experience chronic joys can break free of traditional limits to lead lives with more choice and freedom. The models for joy enable human beings to be free right now despite their circumstances. Distinguishing between joy and other human experiences helps us to define joy.

DISTINGUISHING BETWEEN JOY AND OTHER HUMAN EXPERIENCES

Human happiness is closely related to joy. One difference is in relationship to clock time and intensity. Happiness is a view of life in total. Happiness includes all human emotions examining the anger, guilt, anxiety, and fear with an accepting and affirming attitude. Joy is describing one slice of life with the beam of a flashlight. Happiness is an overall picture of life illuminated by a searchlight. Joy is intense, limited in time and space. Joy is an immediate celebration of a moment in time that has significance and value. It involves intense ego interest. Examples we would give if asked would be the birth of a child, being healed of cancer or a serious illness, an unexpected reward, or being rescued from eminent danger. Hearing or reading about joy experiences causes us to want to share ours with others.

Happiness is an attitude or view of living that does not depend on outside forces to sustain it. The key thought is that happiness is within us. It is an inner force that reminds us of the happy life we have lived. Some of us might say at the end of our days, "I wish I had realized it earlier. I would have enjoyed it more." What a wealth we could build for our world if we would enjoy every possible minute of our own lives. One way to record our happiness is to journal every day. We could then see that if we are in a down time, a deep valley, we will likely be on a hill with another time of joy coming soon.

Starting this minute we can begin discovering the potential for more happiness within ourselves. We must make up our mind to journey on that upward course not wavering from our determined purpose.

We can form our viewpoint by seeking the positives in living rather than denying the joyful by moaning about the bad as most of us do. When we stop playing that game of "life is awful," go inside yourself and ask, "How can I make each day better for myself and others?" Appreciate and cherish life. Happy people hold dearly to the gift of time with respect and joyful anticipation. They regard every hour as extremely valuable for their productive purposes. Happiness means telling your muscles to move, to get out of our beds of retreat and ease. If we focus on depression and dreariness, we are living half-dead, missing out on all the beauty that now lives. In spite of all the pain, rejections, and struggles realize that every one of those moments lived through the valley experiences got us to the hill, this joyful moment. We can make the decision to tell our muscles to move so that we will be determined survivors.

We can train ourselves to not listen to everything the brain tries to tell us. We can sustain a sense of joyful anticipation so intense that we can hardly wait for a day to begin so that you can exert your wakeful efforts to enjoy the day, each day, completely. We might recall how Shakespeare described a person of hope: "The sun shall not be up so soon as I try the fair adventure of tomorrow."

Take this first step. We must do it. Wealth begins with the saved penny. A wealth of joy and happiness begins with shared joys. The longest journey cannot begin until we take a first step. Happiness is an inside job. It comes from our contacts with others and reflects its benefits on them and on us all.

A second step would be to develop attitudes and abilities which result in the joy-filled life. Inner realization and moving of your mouth, feet, hands, arms, and brain muscles form the key to a positive happy life and moments of joy. Perhaps it is an overused statement but remember today is the first day of the rest of your life. Millions of our cells are reborn each day. Every day we must begin a rediscovery of our world. What will today bring for us?

Finding ways to create a happy outlook will enable us to make the most of today and tomorrow and all the years ahead. Never focus on the end. We cannot change the past not matter what we do. It's gone away, never to return. Focus on our beginnings.

During this healing attitudes step, recognize all the clues to gaining even the slightest happiness from each day. We have all heard about the little optimistic boy who was doing the job of shoveling manure inside a barn. He said, "Heck, I enjoy doing this job. There has to be a pony in here someplace."

DISTINGUISHING BETWEEN PLEASURE AND JOY

Don't confuse short-term pleasure from external sources with joy. True and lasting joy always comes from within. External pleasures never last. One way to distinguish between pleasure and joy is that pleasure has a body focus. Washing our hair, enjoying a vigorous backrub, rubbing on lotion, holding hands, sleeping under clean sheets, kissing lips, feeling clean clothes, eating tasty foods, or sitting in a comfortable chair are activities that focus on the wellbeing of our bodies.

Jouissance, the French word for excessive joy, derives from the verb jouir meaning to enjoy, or to have extreme or deep pleasure. Jouissance is contrasted with the word plaisir which means pleasure linked to cultural enjoyment. Jouissance is distinguished from pleasure. Julia Kristeva offers a slight development and a bit of wordplay: she uses plaisir for sexual pleasure and jouissance as a total joy-moment due to the presence of meaning. If a sexual moment has the elements of surprise, ego enhancement, reality, caring, orgasmic delight, spirituality, and meaning, than a sexual experience could be a joy experience. The Song of Solomon is a grand example. So is the mysticism, rapture, and sensuality found in the spiritual writings of Hildegard of Bingen.

Sometimes humans seek pleasure to avoid reality. Drugs and alcohol give pleasure. But as chemicals are abused, guilt sleeps and joy becomes dull. Anxiety becomes tranquilized. Fear hides, and anger unloosens. Giving in to pleasure dulls our emotional responses to give us another perception of reality.

Depression, lethargy, and despair follow quickly from short-lived pleasure for those who abuse the body. Joy involves reality. Pleasure gives a false or distorted sense of reality. Joy is rare. Pleasure occurs often.

We could spend time describing elation, satisfaction, euphoria, moods, or other life experiences. Feel free to do it now.

Our thoughts from outside stimuli include facts and the emotional instincts brought to the facts. We are not in control of the facts of life, things that pop into our lives. We can choose how to respond emotionally to those facts. If we choose positive instincts, we will know happiness. If we choose negative emotional instincts, we'll be unhappy. Happiness depends on what emotions we choose to experience and how we live our lives.

Positive emotion creates an atmosphere for sheer happiness and times of joy.

If we have degrees of jealousy, hate, greed, guilt, or fear, we immediately lower our brain chemistry and our ability to reason and function at an excellent level. Our negative emotional instincts are the cause of most of our bad decisions, impulsive actions, and unhappiness. Bad chemistry yields lack of self-awareness and ignorance.

GO WHERE THE JOY IS

We have no clear maps as to just where and when joy will come into our lives. We are just told to go where the joy is. If we had a map of our journeys to joy, we would be able to know when to tread lightly and when to stomp wildly.

Most mornings we wake up hoping we will be able to control the outcome of the day before us. Some mornings we wake up longing for a way to go back to start, the start of yesterday or the start of last week or the start of twenty years ago, the start of whatever led to the day with which we are about to struggle. We fantasized about going back to the start. Perhaps we will avoid being in a car accident, being fired, losing a spouse, showing fired-up anger to a friend, or missing out on something. We just wish that we could superimpose today's wisdom over yesterday's *faux pas*. We wish that we didn't have to wake up to the doubt and despair that often makes its home in our lives.

All of us have been engaged at one time or another in the struggle to save ourselves from our regrets and our pain. Where is the joy as we leave undone those things that we should have done and we have done those things that we ought not to have done. We know that we cannot go back to the start.

Life has to be lived in the now moments. Every moment is precious. Go where the joy is. Go where the desire to live the life that is laid out before us, both certainties and uncertainties, over the desire to sanitize or amend what we have left undone or what we ought not to have done. Life has many holes in the road. We must live in the present, and that's where the joy is. It's in the uncertain journey. Joy might be found as we calm ourselves and capture the beauty of nature. Joy is where we accept the tension between our willing spirits and the uncooperative early morning plan of anticipation. To go where the joy is implies to recognize that life is about to happen again. We learn and live by going where we have to go.

Each moment that we are awakened to now opportunities or the urge to be present gives us the directions to where the joy is. That journey of getting where we have to go will be wrought with detours. We have to take a right on Doubt Street. We turn left at Disappointment Avenue. Drive out of one cul-de-sac and into another. We run out of our expensive gasoline on Transition Boulevard. We have experienced these frustrations on past journeys and we will experience these frustrations again. The detours are why we leave our every day environment and routine and head for the woods. We never avoid the detours, the congestion, and potholes on our ways, but being together is how we refuel and how we make the crooked places straight. Those on that uncertain journey with us are our sources for joy.

It is impossible for us to have too much joy. Joy is the most fulfilling, the healthiest of all human emotions. Attempting to contain our joy can only result in an environment in our lives that will cause a loss of the joy response. Nobody ever enjoyed their selves to death.

Jouissance is about embracing time. Excessive and spontaneous joy will bless every moment of our human experiences.

PRACTICAL APPLICATION

Compare books written about joy by psychiatrists and psychologists with those by entertainers and preachers. Note their words and the contradictions found in the books.

List some advantages to living in chronic joy. Begin with these positive factors:

- Joy stimulates our immune system
- Joy gives us personal power
- Joy enhances mental ability
- Joy fosters creativity
- Joy enables us to be emotionally present
- Joy increases energy
- Joy helps us live longer
- *

What messages did you receive did you receive from your childhood family about joy and happiness?

*

*

*

*

*

*

*

*

*

*

V

EMBRACING TIME

Oh, this is the joy of the rose: That it blows, and goes.

— Willa Cather

W HEN WE HAVE SUFFERED A valley experience, people expect us to bounce back to a hilltop experience soon, sooner than we are able. They need us to because they have trouble being with us when we are depressed. In terms of our own experience of time, we expect ourselves to bounce back quickly. We demand it, but our bodies and minds insist on taking us first on that journey through darkness and rage, the valley of loneliness and pain.

Before mechanical timepieces were invented, people organized their lives with the natural events of light and dark, the seasons, and the tides. Some of the events were predictable as the moving of the sun and moon. The sunset was highly regular, but it gets dark on cloudy days earlier than on a clear day. One event of nature shaded into another. Tides come and go gradually. Spring could come slowly. This natural way of telling time gave a cushion that is different from the sound of the alarm clock going off at exactly six o'clock. Work starts at exactly eight or nine o'clock and stops at exactly five or six o'clock. The cushion in telling time enabled early humans to work more at their own pace. They took time to find what needed to be accomplished each time period. The time was a cyclical time. Mechanical time passes and never returns. Day follows day, spring follows spring, one year follows another year. The consequences of not realizing the time for a season were severe. The early humans did not always have food for the winter, or it might be too late to plant for a full harvest. If early humans could make it through winter, there would be another opportunity. Time will come around again.

We measure time more accurately than it has ever been measured. Ordinary digital wristwatches are calibrated in hundredths of a second. These inexpensive watches are accurate within a few seconds each month. Expensive watches are ever better and more precise. Every child is fascinated with the clock. One of our first presents that we request from parents is a watch. Some of us even wear our Mickey Mouse watches into old age. All this scientific control of time does not seem to make us happier. We are more efficient. Workplaces can control when we are there, in a building or at a desk. Something in the way we can now control time causes less quality of time. The quantity is assured; the quality might be missing.

REVIEWING OUR LIFE VIDEOS

Some theologians tell us that after death, we can review our whole lifetime of hills and valleys, good times and bad times, and that we will be enabled to see and understand the consistency of God's working through all things for our good. Unexpected meanings will be revealed in those after-life videos of the brief time we human beings spend on earth. And our sense of time will be different. Maybe we will have the perception that "a thousand years is as a day" as God views time. We will clearly understand how a pattern joining things together that seemed to us to be unrelated.

We will then understand that our past impatience was fruitless. We will see clearly, not as through a dark glass, because we will comprehend that there was simply no way to hurry the process.

Impatience doesn't make the valley time easier. It does make it worse. We get frustrated and angry with ourselves for not winning over the sorrow. We think this valley time will never end. We lose hope thinking we'll never be in a joy again. We lose the perspective that a hill experience always follows the valley time. We begin to think that our emotional agony will not lift. People tell us this down time will end, but nobody can tell us exactly when. Will it end tomorrow, next week, next year? If we could see our valley in God's view of time, it would have a similar effect. The pace of things in life would appear as being exactly correct. We would also have the insight that we could have changed it somewhat. In fact, because we could attend to critical tasks that we are now not aware of, and are in our time and perception, neglecting, we would see what is happening to us, and we would be content with God's care of us during our valleys.

Joy is in love with life. Joy is spontaneous and at the same time immensely patient. In a joy we realize that there are sharp rocks along every path. Still every moment is a perfect moment. Joy is not demanding, cares not a wit for success or failure or making the jouissance permanent. During passionate joy, time stands still.

Healing is a long and gradual process. Climbing out of a valley time includes living with memories of joys. Realistically, we cannot offer comfort. People have to embrace this valley of pain and tears. We give those in the valley time space to experience the shock, startle, or horror of their loss. After a funeral, we eat. Although in the valley, we need to return to see new possibilities for happiness. Embracing the doldrums times—times of job loss, divorce, illness, pain—is to embrace loss of security, status, lifestyle, health, and confidence. All valley times need us to embrace their reality.

Our desire for joy in our starving world causes us to want instant gratification. We want a McDonald's meal now. We use the Home Shopping Network, a fast diet plan, and the Concorde jet. We join an exercise club to get muscles in a month. Plastic surgeons promise instant, eternal beauty. Television evangelists promise salvation with a touch of the hand. We cannot speed through suffering. No therapist, drug, or psychic can prevent us from experiences in the valley times. Every moment in the present, even those of valley times, offers an opportunity to gain new awareness.

This day will have 24 hours in it. The same time is measured out for each person. Kings, presidents, and beggars get the same number of hours. The next year will have its usual number of days, and then it's over. What we do during these days is another matter. The model we use today is understood exclusively in terms of numbers. Is it better to live our lives here on earth with our time perceptions, even though that time of life can be sustained by machines and be completely unproductive?

We talk about "good" days and "bad" days. What we mean is their length. We know that a nice summer day is not "better" than a short, cold winter day. The value of a day depends on what we do with it, or with what kind of human experience we have on the day. Was last year a good one for us? We have little control over what kind of year we'll have. It might have many valleys and low times, or it could be full of hills, high times of quality and human accomplishment. With God we need to ask, "What did we learn? What has happened to our relationships with one another, with other families, with other institutions, with other nations? How has life changed?"

Most of us never reflect on the skills we need to get out of the doldrums. We merely slide into a cocooning time. We don't prepare so that when it is time to "go for it," we merely live. We walk, talk, love, hate, and die a little each day without embracing the processes. Embracing all time keeps us ageless. Feeling life in the times of hills as well as valleys is the most valuable beauty secrets we can possess.

Will next year be a good one for us? We have little control over most of the surprising events that will come our way. Will the time go smoothly or will we have unforeseen difficulties. The essential "goodness" of our coming years will depend on our responses.

The times of the year will come with choices. Some of our choices will involve the choices of differing actions. Sometimes we will not have much of a choice in what will happen or how we'll respond to the event. We can only do our best.

Sometimes this means just a little insight. A family in Lincoln, Nebraska, bought a house in a wooded area near the shore of a lake. For years they complained that their view from the living room was restricted because the window was too narrow. Their daughter told them, "Open it up." When they did, the new window revealed lovely trees, colorful flowers, blue water and reflected sky. The family's spirits were lifted each new day.

Moving our muscles and opening our minds from the moment of waking up each day will help us see that day as new and untouched. Our responsibility is to create an atmosphere to make the days pleasant rather than trying experiences. Instead of viewing our living as something to *beware*, we accept the challenge to *be aware*. We can function with all our senses open, being alert, awake, and receptive. Try an exercise in awareness:

Look as though your eyesight might dim at any minute. Listen as if your ears would fail at any time and close out all sounds, a loved one's voice, a bird's song, or music. Touch with the possibility that at any instant we could lose our ability to feel. Use the senses avidly as though they might desert us in a split second in time. Exert and profit from the natural exercises that come with humming, singing, laughter, whistling. Build lung function. It's part of building our wealth of joy.

EMBRACING TIME MEANS TO ACCEPT OUR LIFE SITUATION

Our road might be a long and difficult one. Anger is a natural response to suffering. We feel so angry, and we can find no one to blame. Finally, we just say hat nobody is to blame, but everybody has to embrace this down in the valley time. We are cruelest to those who are closest to us and they absorb much of our rage. We turn on our friends for the simple reason that they are happy and not suffering the way we are suffering. If some much loved and needed person dies, we resent that person who died for abandoning us. Also, we turn our anger on ourselves. We hate ourselves for being weak, unable to bounce back from our valley. We hate God for not preventing the tragedy that fell upon us, for not responding to our prayers. Valley times heal slowly.

Another common response to valley times is a desire to return to the past. Anything seems better than facing the unknown road that lies before us. When we feel lost, even certain torment might seem better than an uncertain future. Battered wives run away from their torture-filled homes only to return to abusive husbands because the pain of surviving on their own was too much to bear. Men and women return to jobs that were crushing their spirits because any alternate path was too uncertain.

Valley times can teach us endurance. Our souls were made for endurance. And valley times enable our faith. If we keep our eyes open in valley times, life will begin to take shape before us. We can learn things about ourselves that we never thought possible. We can uncover wisdom and compassion that has remained dormant during our times in the doldrums. We can find strength that is eternal and never ending. We can carry these lessons of our valley times into every day of our lives.

SOME THINGS ARE BEYOND OUR CONTROL

No matter what we have lost during our times of life, there is always something that survives with which to start over. There is always some shred of hope, some way to begin again, to go for it. Life is fragile and unpredictable. Life does not always go the way we would like it to go. We only have to look at the hills and valleys of our own lives to understand this truth. Make a chart of your life from the year of your birth. Take a sheet of paper. Draw a line from left to right across the page. Begin with your year of birth. At five-year intervals write a note of whether a time of hills or valleys happened. Place the hills in the top half, valleys in the lower half. Most of us will be encouraged to have the insight that nobody has all hill times or valley times. All that we own can be taken away in an instant. But all of us have the power to start over, to trust again, for finding another job, to carry our confidence and our faith wherever our journey takes us.

Our life charts will tell us that after we have confronted the valleys and gained strength from the comforts and joys of our high moments, we must begin the process of rebuilding the real wealth of our lives. This is not easy. For some of us, it is downright overwhelming. Where do we begin? How can we go where the joy is if we don't have a clue where life will take us? When will our lives begin again?

A southern California family built their new home right on the spot of their old home that burned to the ground during a fire. Why would they build in that same spot? They noted that walking away from their property would be to admit defeat, to stay in a valley of fear. Every time they smell smoke, they think that perhaps another fire is coming through their valley. But they rebuilt despite their fears. And they nailed a silver medal that adorned their old house. It read, "God bless our home."

SLOWING DOWN TO REFRESH OURSELVES

Slowing down to give our lives pace and balance does not happen automatically. We have to move our muscles to take the initiative. We must stop and enjoy the pause that refreshes us.

When we are transitioning to this change of pace, it helps to inquire of ourselves by asking a few questions about our use of time.

First, what is the cost in time of our actual involvements? Is it worth our precious time? Is what we are doing an expression of our purpose in life? Is this a faithful respond to what the grace of living asks of us?

Then, what is our strategy for slowing down? What works

best for each of us as an individual? Do we need a nap? Would we enjoy walking in the woods? Would we enjoy talking to our children or grandchildren?

There is no such thing as time management. All of us have the same amount of time. We need to learn priority management. Only we can determine what we must be doing to fulfill our individual mission for life. Set and reset priorities and stick to them in the light of your personal values. Return frequently to reflect and think about our life vocation and whatever it asks from us. Instead of fretting about how much you can get done in so much time, ask who we are as a world neighbor and as a person. Think in these times what we can create for ourselves. Appraise all the activities. Can any be given up for the sake of regaining your freedom from the distress of doing? Do these activities add to our fulfillment, our happiness, or our moments when joy enters our lives?

Weed out all the wasted activity that takes away from your life purpose. Some of us do too much aimless socializing. We are clued to the television for countless hours, numbing our creativity. We run silly errands and travel to see things just to stay busy. We engage in hours of window-shopping that are unconnected to our purposes. We make unnecessary telephone calls to escape loneliness or silence. Cell phones are in the hands of every teen and especially those who drive automobiles. We lose much time in idle gossip and meaningless gossip.

Preoccupation with time can take joy from our lives. Joy doesn't wear a watch but always gets to essential places on time. Become aware of how often we look at our watches. How frequently do we look at the clock on the wall? In school we wait for the bell to ring out the information that class is over. How much of our time-checking is necessary? How much is just compulsive or neurotic? Do you abuse time? Enjoy games in a noncompetitive fashion. Cultivate a genuine interest in playing with your children. Put time for fun into your calendar. Make quilts, pottery, art pieces.

Pay attention to your body's inner clock. How does sunlight or lack of it affect us? How about change of temperature? How much sleep do you need to function at your best? What is your temperament like? What stresses you to the point of anger? Do you have a short fuse when under pressure? Can you take much stress and still produce?

All of us have experienced times of flow. At these times we produce more and enjoy these peak periods of production. Too often we offer to our children an example of frantic rushing. How wonderful to cause the next generation to relax. And we'll be on our way to a healthy life with times of joy. And this joy we feel will clear the environment around us. *Jouissance* will uplift our heavy hearts. It is unlikely that chronic stress but sheer joy will prevail when we live in this way.

REVIVING OUR PASSIONS OF YESTERDAY

What are three things you'd like to do someday? What passions did you write down in your diary or journal five or ten years ago? Could someday be done today? Is it time to revive those yearnings?

Happiness is realized on a day-to-day basis. We have our time in this world. And if we live it again in our memories, our time will reward us with wisdom. We will come to understand our life as a whole event. Some of our decisions that we were not aware of making will be significant life choices. So we dispassionately rejoice in the good ones and regret the poor ones.

Sharing photos or journals of time passed can revive us

today. Friends and family can give us the push we need to move our muscles. Of course, most of us will need to find support and reinforcement. Seek that support from your intimates now. And now just who believes in you more than you do in yourself?

Shirley Maclaine said, "I think of life now as a wonderful play that I've written for myself. So my purpose is to have the utmost fun playing my part."

MAKING THE JOY CONNECTION

We were created with the capacity to connect with joy. We journey through our days in a dull trance, asleep to the magic happening all around us. Joy waits for each of us. Joy's desire to walk with us is far greater than our longing to accompany this delightful emotion.

After reading about building your wealth of joy, can you remember some of your personal joy times? Now think how they brought surprising commitment and clarity, exhilaration and encounter. These ego-enhancing times when you felt excessively alive as you offered thanks without prompting can be revisited in the videos of your mind.

What is your first memory of a joy experience?

During that *jouissance* you experienced a miracle. You knew an epiphany, an ah-ha point in time when the static of the world cleared. In a joy, you understood that Morse code of your inner being, so many times dismissed as meaningless or not possible. You connected to joy on your deepest level.

A visitor was passing by a building site. He wondered what the workers were building. "What are you doing?" he asked one of them. "I'm digging a whole," he replied. He asked another worker, "What are you doing?" That workman said, "I'm mix-

ing cement." He asked a third person. That one said, "I'm building a wall."

As he asked a fourth worker, he sensed a light of interest
in his eyes. This one smiled as he declared, "We're building a
cathedral."

MUNDANE, TRIVIAL, OR ETERNAL LIFE

As we contemplate our days, our years of living on this
planet, we must raise our thinking from the trivial and mundane
to the eternal. Time is not a treadmill for satisfying our material
wants and our self-led pleasures. Time is a spiritual staircase
leading upward with its final part of the journey ending in joy.
We can use our time to transform our lives by moving from the
dull doldrums and the tedium of animal existence to the beauty
and energy of living. We can suffuse the human space around
us with the unconditional love and brightness of wisdom. Building a wealth of joy that cannot be taken from us or left after our
time of earth has gone requires a deep understanding of the
deep realities of life, so that as we think about the years in front
of us, whether they be few or they be many, we view this time
as continual opportunities to grow closer to each other with
mutual understanding that will create an eternal use of life.

CHANGING OR PUTTING AWAY NEGATIVE VIDEOS

Those videos we keep in our brains have been there since
birth. Why do we think and act like we do? Even just six months
after conception, when we are still in our mother's wombs, our
brains start recording our mothers' thoughts and actions.

Our brain continues to record our personal life videos for the rest of our lives. Our videos are a record of our entire history, all our thoughts and actions. The importance of those videos is that we are programmed to make decisions according to what is on our past videos.

Those videos show our weaknesses and our strengths. Your videos are there to keep us at our present level within our comfort zones. Our actions and our thoughts of this moment are a reflection of what is on a past video. Some of our current beliefs were placed in our personal video shelves by our parts and by our social conditioning. We placed these videos in our library of the mind and accepted them as our own. Our present level of happiness and the number of joy videos we own are a reflection of our atmosphere of past thoughts and actions. We can become aware of what's on those videos. It is critical to view these to understand our personal design.

When we attempt to change, we have to overcome what is on some of our life videos. Our videos make it easy to repeat what we have thought and done in our pasts. We have to move our muscles to increase our determination to change. Our mind videos do not care whether we are positive or negative, happy or unhappy. They are only concerned with having us repeat our past thoughts and actions.

It's not bad to have all those videos in our minds. Without those videos, we would have no memories. We would not know our name or our identity, how to talk, or anything else we have learned. That's why diseases of the brain and mind are so devastating. We have no database for living.

We and our social conditioning, our wounds, and our accumulation of negative thoughts and actions hold us back. To change our life atmosphere, we have to find out what is on our life videos. We won't change overnight. Give yourself time.

Strengthen your desire to change. Move your muscles.

BE GENTLE WITH YOURSELF

If you do decide that you would like more happiness and joy, but you keep repeating the same mistakes and negative behavior, don't become depressed or beat yourself up. Learn to laugh at yourself. Laughter is your best friend. Acknowledge that you own all those negative videos. The videos contain what honestly is everything about you. The brain will respond to your muscles, your efforts to change. Some of those videos were placed in your library by other people. But we accept them as our own.

Our happiness is a reflection of what is on our life videos. We have to accept them, even if they cause us to be uncomfortable. Moving our muscles helps us to understand that we can become in control of our personal videos. We have to work smarter and harder to change what we can.

We can gain enough wisdom and insight to overcome our video's control over us. We can change those past tendencies because the most recent videos have the biggest impact on our decision-making.

Using our thinking muscles creates a war between our desire to change and our video's strong influence. When faced with something life threatening such as cancer, we change our behavior. Our strong desire to live gives us strength to overcome our videos of the past. The more we understand our videos in our minds. Then, we can sense what is holding us back. Our brain needs to know how to respond in the future. By recording new thoughts and new actions on our videos consistently, your brain begins to show us new habits. We can increase our positive thinking, our joy instinct, to enhance our brain chemistry and natural ability to experience the joy response.

PRACTICAL APPLICATION

Write down some things that have created negative videos in your life's library, those things that are *joy killers.*

Make a list of our joy killers. Some suggestions:

1. Loss of hope. How many victims of hurricanes or other disasters found loss of hope?

2. A rigid, critical childhood family

3. Lack of connection with other people, lack of trusting or intimacy

4. Fear of losing control

5. Poor self-esteem

6. Belief that we don't deserve joy

7. Assumption that extrinsic things such as possessions can make us happy

8. Fear of taking risks

9. Spiritual doubts

10. Lack of trust in self—doubting our decisions and perceptions in life

11. Working to avoid feeling or facing problems, driven to work

12. Inability to be emotionally present with others

13. Fear of joy

14. Shame based addictions such as substance abuse, sex, food

15. Childhood trauma

16. Domestic violence

17. Mental disorders or belonging to a mentally ill family

18. Identify your own joy killers . . .

VI

APPRECIATING YOUR
PERSONALITY

A thing of beauty is a joy forever.

— John Keats

OUR UNIQUE PERSONALITIES WILL influence the ways we respond to life situations. There are many psychological instruments that enable us to appreciate what kind of personalities we prefer. The Myers-Briggs Personality Inventory has been used to enable people to understand themselves and others. Colors, birth order, family environment, and other psychological or spiritual instruments are used to help us put these ideas to use. We can then have some idea about who we are and who other people are, and we can better understand them.

We are all unique, with differences that need to be appreciated if our time on earth has meaning. We are often attracted to others by the ways they are different from us. But those differences can later become sources of irritation and discontent.

For example, early in a relationship, we might feel that we really like the fact that another person is outgoing or assertive. Later, we might regard such assertiveness as being controlling. Opposites attract, but opposites have to work harder to maintain relationships.

We become tired of the differences and long for the day when another person would think like we think, believe as we believe, react like we would react, and want the things we want.

Differences are felt so keenly that we want to escape the relationship altogether. It's just too much work. We might just think about a relationship we need to work on. In what way is that other person hurting right now? And what could we do to ease the suffering and restore a sense of happiness and times for joy.

We can take pride in our attributes such as our sensitivity, awareness, and wisdom. We have much to give if we would just be willing to give. We have much to gain by honoring our individuality. And we can enjoy our unique gifts. No one person is better than another. Never put yourself down. Flaws and faults can be corrected, not exaggerated or dwelled upon. Pride yourself on your positive characteristics. None should demand perfection. Our justified pride will become us and lead us to more consciousness and appreciation. Joy times and happiness are found within us.

SEEKING AND FINDING OUR PERSONAL TRUTH

Rebuilding our lives requires us to accept that something is broken.

Some of us respond to misfortune by refusing to accept our brokenness. Determination leads us to overcome adversity. The only way to heal ourselves is to accept the truth we have denied.

Of course, there are difficult valleys in life that we will never be able to circumvent. No effort on our part will change things. Some valleys will continue and these low times will refuse to bend to our desires. What will we do when there is no way out? Why do we place so much emphasis on the power of the will? To assume that we have ultimate power to determine our destiny is a form of idolatry. Physical or mental illnesses do not find cures from our having the correct mind-set. We have to empower people to climb out of their valleys. Just how do we communicate that message for people on their deathbeds? Do they fail? Did they not try enough?

No outside force can cure schizophrenia or bipolar disorder.

John Killinger tells of a schizophrenic friend who says she actually loves the moment when she's slipping from one personality to another. She has such fantastic insights at that time. Many of the world's great art and insights in music and literature have come from schizophrenic and bipolar episodes.

Bipolarity teaches us the wonderful buoyancy of grace, that won't let us sink even when we try, but keeps returning us to the top. Our most intimate and caring supporters help us realize that with all the lifetimes of suffering and rejection, we keep sinking to the top.

No force of will can create a cure. The most faithful act for us then is to realize that our healing is not in our power. We can do all that medical science has told us to do, but we must find joy despite our illness. We can want something with all our wills. We can expend all our energy trying to find it, and still things will not go our way.

Joy happens within relationships with other people. Sometimes a relationship just cannot ever happen as we'd desire it. We can never force another to change or to love us. All we can do is to accept what is before us and try to make the best of our situations. Over time we can stop searching for a change in reality or a transformation of another person. Only then can we stop searching for something we will never find. Only then can we put our best efforts into looking for comfort and happiness and even moments of sheer joy where they can be found, in other people, our friends, our communities, and within ourselves.

No amount of effort or preparation can keep an illness at bay. Tragedies come to those who are good or evil. Some lovely people are just out of reach for us. We have to accept and respect that some are already married or in a relationship or that they are not capable of love or caring. That is not to believe that we must just give in to whatever life's journey takes us without a struggle. Not for a moment. But we do have to learn when to try to change our situation and when just to accept the reality, even if it is unfair.

Denying reality will not shield us from disappointment and pain. This denial prevents us from moving forward. It just prolongs self-defeating behavior. Only when we admit to ourselves that we cannot save an awful marriage or find a fulfilling job are we ready to move on with our lives. Only when we learn to accept things as they are can we find the insight to improve our lives. Each of us has known valley times when we just had to let go of the urge to control. There are times when we welcome the death of a marriage, a job, or life itself.

There are valley times when we must discover the courage to embrace the many times of death instead of fighting them. No amount of anger will change the reality of our losses. Giving up the struggle will lead us to enormous relief. Only then can we begin to grief our losses, saying goodbye and expressing gratitude for the joyful moments shared in the high times when the relationship, the job, the joy was real.

On our journeys we hope people will accept us and care

for us despite our frailties, our contradictions, and idiosyncrasies. In our seeking and finding of ourselves, we shall surely discover that others have them too. Events that are beyond our control are painful and tragic. But there is another side to our sad moments. Our world is as vast and as changeable as the people who inhabit our planet. As frustrating as this is, it can be a source of comfort or even inspiration. In a world where anything can happen is a world where joy-filled things can happen. Our diverse world is a world where joy and love will surprise us when we are not even searching for it. Kindness can come from the least likely places. Unexpected discoveries can be made that will cure illnesses and preserve life. War can give way to peace. Miracles happen. Hurts are healed. Work bears fruit. Our dreams of a better world become realties.

We have been running and hiding far too long. We are tired, incomplete, and weary. We must face the truth about ourselves that we cannot deny. Ignoring our pain will not make it go away. We need courage to confront what we have feared to face. We need this kind of courage to endure what we cannot escape.

Personal truth is within ourselves, but frequently it is clouded by other motivations and inner subterfuges, so that we have to dig deep inside ourselves to find our clear personal truth. Our truth has to be without self-delusions and without hiding any actuality from ourselves.

Seeking and finding basic, simple truth—simple because all pretexts have been removed—can be the most satisfying feelings in life. If we lie to ourselves or if we deceive ourselves, we know it and so do other people. From that viewpoint, we will doubt our ability to recognize and share the truth to anybody. Removing self-deception is like ripping away a distorting veil that clouds our vision and irritates us so we cannot function in happiness and times of joy. When we have unloaded the weight of self-deception we will find a liberating understanding of ourselves and others. Sensing this energizing freedom will cause us to wonder, "Why didn't we enjoy such clarity before this time?"

Finding our personal truth includes knowing who we are, what we really are seeking on life's journey, without self-concealment, will open us to reach towards a higher level of life. Having accepted our personal truths, we can look ourselves in the mirror and say, "I am no longer one of the untouchables."

We who have endured the depressive doldrums, the times of cocooning, the periods of preparing for our next adventure, and then we go for it. During one time period we define ourselves as completely normal, protected, safe from the chuckholes along our personal journeys. During our next phase we become the target of one of life's cruel blows. We are now the injured, the rejected, the victims, the unemployed, and the sick. We can no longer view suffering as the fate of those people who cling to misfortune and daily pain. Now it is our inheritance. People begin to talk about us with pity and relief that we never visualized could come our way. They speak of us with pity, because they cannot feel our pain. They speak with relief, because they are pleased that it is we who have to endure the agony and not them.

If our personal truth is that we are compulsive liars and our conscience reminds us to tell the truth, forgiving ourselves for lying is not enough. We must choose to break the habit by telling the truth. We must be willing to change behaviors to embrace our personal truth.

Personal truth brings integrity. Integrity is that which produces wholeness in our lives. Integrity is the result of integrating our personal truth into our everyday behavior. Lack of integrity disintegrates wholeness. Without integrity, our lives fall apart.

Conscience can be the whispers of angels to tell us what is good for us, what will make us happy and to know those precious moments of joy.

FAILURE, SUFFERING, AND GRIEF ENTER INTO OUR LIVES IN AN INSTANT

Our world can change dramatically overnight. Nothing is as it was. Lifelong friends desert us. Professional colleagues try to make believe that nothing has happened.

Relationships are thrown into turmoil. Our self-images are shattered.

And so we have to redefine our true selves. We who have hit a bump in life's journey, at some point, search through the process of redefining ourselves. We want to continue to pretend that nothing has changed for us. When we try to erase or deny that we have suffered a blow, the blow can end up as a source of secrecy and shame, of disgrace and humiliation. Somehow in our heart of hearts, we know we should not be embarrassed by our misfortune. Having been hurt is not a sign of weakness. For some people, hurts are signs of strength.

Happy people who experience times of joy have to be willing to say to themselves and others: "I have a mental illness," "I am a person whose marriage failed," or "I am an orphan." It is healthy to embrace the full force of these words. The words do not define who we are, but they define a part of our personal truth that we can face and acknowledge.

The times in the valleys of failure, suffering, and grief are difficult as we accept new self-definitions, as we identify ourselves among the wounded. When we can accept ourselves as the vulnerable humans that we are, we will find this new identity is less frightening than we have imagined. It is easier to live with personal truths than it is to live with personal lies.

Truth is that we who walk around feeling invulnerable are the ones who are fooling themselves. It is terrifying to learn that we are helpless to prevent these times of pain and agony. But the wisdom we gain from these valley times can help us to appreciate our lives in a way we could never have known. When life experiences teach us that lives can be shattered in an instant, we learn to treat each day with reverence. We no longer take our joy moments for granted.

We appreciate them as precious gifts. When we become connected to another person who needs our help, the pity we would have shown is replaced by empathy. Distance is replaced with understanding. Our callousness is replaced by love. Suddenly we are aware of how we can help. We are no longer tongue-tied. We are not uncomfortable. We can look another person who is in pain right into the eye and say, "I know. I have been there."

OUR STORIES REVEAL THE VICTIMS AND THE VICTORS

Helen Teisher has been called the founding mother of mental health advocacy. She died of bone cancer in 2004 at age 86. Her calling was to open minds for recognition of the needs of the mentally ill. She called on state and national legislators to help battle the myths that have stigmatized generations of dysfunctional families. Her vision included halfway houses and socialization centers. Her calling to heal the mentally ill was so energized that more than 500 people joined her local San Diego chapter. She used every skill, even quilting exquisite creations to raise funds to support the cause. Helen was a teacher whose vocal witness as an advocate for mental health sufferers. The American Psychiatric Association awarded her the coveted Warren Williams Foundation Award. An active woman, she spoke to many national and international groups on behalf of those struck with mental illness.

In the Netherlands, a group of miners were working underground when the mine where they were working collapsed. They could not dig themselves out. All of them were aware that eventually in time their oxygen would run out.

These Dutch miners had no idea how long the underground oxygen supply would last. All they could do was to sit and wait to be rescued. Time, suddenly, was of the essence. Time, suddenly, was all these miners could think about. Time, suddenly, meant everything.

Only one miner was wearing a watch. They had the desire to know exactly how long they would be in the closed-in mine shaft. They wanted to know the hours spent waiting for the oxygen to run out for them. The man with the watch volunteered to call out each hour.

Each hour that he announced the time, the miners panicked more and more, anxiety levels went through the roof. They sweated tears of fearful anger. To help them in their mental plight, the man called out one hour for every two that he knew had passed. He tried to slow down the time.

Six days later, rescue workers finally reached the miners. Such joy came to each miner who came out alive. Only one man died. It was the one with the watch.

The only man who truly knew just how long they had been trapped in the mineshaft died.

Each human season, each life event, every place of healing serves to sharpen our possibilities and to underline our uniqueness. Stories are never typical. There is no predictable or typical life journey. There is no such thing as an ordinary pathway. Frederick Buechner once said, "My assumption is that the story of one of us is in some measure the story of us all."

Our own stories have been paralyzed by our pain, our cynicism, not feeling feelings, and our ugliness. We have believed that we have been so ugly, so weak, and so inept that we have rejected ourselves. We hate to be around others when we are this way, and yet we cannot finish our journey by ourselves. Everything has seemed like one twisted hassle. Some days we feel that we've wasted most of our lives and missed the correct turn in the road.

Who among us has not felt so disconnected and out of sync with our own family that we did not wonder at differing times if the nurses had switched babies at the hospital? Surely your real family would understand the real you. Wouldn't they?

There are only two ways to approach life, as a victim or as a victor. We decide to act or react. We can step into the victim mentality without wanting it or knowing it. There is hope. Our mourning can be turned into dancing and my sackcloth into joy, despite our imperfections. That which appears to us as limitation can become our unexpected advantage and asset. Acceptance of our limits means that we accept the whole process. Acceptance means that we let go of who we think we ought to be so that we can become what we want to be. Our people are not always our family. Unfortunately, we mix them up most of the time. This causes enormous emotional stress and disillusion. Our people are, more than not, our spiritual people. These we unconditionally love and are loved by. Sometimes our people are connected by bloodlines. Some of our people intersect with our lives in order to play a role crucial to enabling us to find our purpose. They could come into our lives for one hour. Some appear and stay in our circle for eternity. Our people might not be welcomed. They push all our buttons and set off every sensor around the perimeter of our sanity. Some people we hate on sight. This person might reflect our personal truth. This person is a mirror reflecting the major flaws in our own personalities that requires our immediate attention.

We define ourselves by what we have, what we wear, what kind of house we live in, or what kind of automobile that we drive. If you think of yourself as the person in the thousand-dollar suit or as the one with the Hermes scarf or the one with a Heisman trophy, a house fire can destroy not only your possessions, but also you.

LIFE CAN CHANGE IN AN INSTANT

A young man was a star long distance runner. One day there was a tingling in his legs. His physician diagnosed multiple sclerosis. He is forced to give up his dream. He pours his suffering onto pages of his journal, and he becomes a published poet.

Moving her body with grace, a ballet dancer twists her ankle and injures herself. She has to stop dancing. Dabbling in photography, her former troupe wants some pictures for a brochure. They enlist her. She knows dance, so she conveys a dancer's energy, beauty, passion, and persistence. The photographs are so brilliant that she now does professional photography. She stumbled upon her joy.

Have you ever done the "house on fire" exercise? The premise is that your house is on fire and you can save only three things. All living creatures, people and animals, have been rescued. What would you save and why?

ACCEPTING OUR DIFFERENCES

The above exercise reveals some of our differences. When differences emerge, we try to make people act like us. None of us are better than others, just different. When we discover differences, we become anxious. Normally, we decide that the cause of the anxiety is the behavior of the other person. Remember Professor Higgins's question, "Why can't a woman be more like a man?" There are differences in every relationship.

And those differences create anxiety and conflicts between us. Friends, parents and their children, coworkers, ethnic groups, labor and management, liberals and conservatives, and nations have to live with differences.

Often, we demand that everybody in our circle be the same. If that happens, then the differing people will respond to us by complying, rebelling, attacking, or cutting off from us. These are ways we react when there is a demand for change. Personalities don't clash in isolation. Never is one person completely the good guy and the other a bad guy. Each of us is just trying to cope with our anxiety about differences and the threats to our human need for closeness or distance from other people. Some will leave or cut off others in their circles. If life gets too tense, they withdraw. Some emotionally disappear, while others will actually leave the house, the city, or even the country. Other persons not as angry, will tune out of conversations, turn on the television, or talk on the cell phone. People can live in the same house and continue to be millions of miles away emotionally.

College students move away from home and make duty visits only when absolutely necessary. We distance because we feel powerless. We might appear to be independent, but that is a façade. The independence depends on our creating emotional distance. Closeness means anxiety or no feelings, not even joy.

As long as they don't become emotionally involved, they can do any job, be social anywhere. Those who are cut off also feel anxiety, fear, and guilt. They think the one who is withdrawing has the power.

Natural differences threaten us, so we demand sameness. To create our wealth in joy, we must study and accept differences. Differing people can develop a personality with a strong sense of self. Knowing ourselves and accepting others' differences is healthy. Differences are positive and they create an atmosphere for surprise, for enabling self-esteem, for building confidence, for finding personal freedom, and for mutual stimulation and growth. Joy will replace the fear and anxiety.

GETTING STUCK IN THE TAR

We who are older might remember the character Brer Rabbit in Joel Chandler Harris's story about the old South. Brer Rabbit hops along the pathway of life, happy, joyful. He is whistling along the road. Suddenly, he encounters a "tar-baby" by the roadside. The tar-baby insults him. Brer Rabbit reacts by going off on the tar-baby. His hand gets stuck in the tar. He tries to hit and kick himself free. Finally he is completely stuck in the tar.

Brer Rabbit thought he was being himself by not letting that tar-baby say nasty things about him. But in fact, he lost sight of his own goals and got embroiled in tar by reacting to another's evaluation of him.

The more we react to other people, the more we lose touch with our purpose and become caught in other people's agendas for us. How can we be close to other people, however different, and not become enmeshed in their opinions, wants, and evaluations?

Therapists use the expression "being differentiated." It means that we can become like a cell in our bodies that separates itself from other cells, but stays in contact. Identifying our own purpose, being one's own self, while continuing a close relationship with others will keep us out of the "tar" that robs us of joy. It is easy to be yourself and to do what you visualize as your unique purpose with people who want what you want. Conflicts happen when one person wants something different from the other. We struggle with the need for sameness as opposed to the need to be a differing individual. When one person's demand for sameness begins to infringe on another's sense of individuality, conflicts are inevitable. All of us want *passionate joy* as we travel life's pathways.

We can be self-differentiated. We can be open about ourselves and accept the differences of others without reaction with negative emotions when others try to change us. We know that changing ourselves does not mean that we have become weak or inadequate. None of us is perfect. We will always be more or less "differentiated" in our relationships. We won't get stuck in a mess of tar. We'll keep on doing what we believe is our own purpose. Others can be different as long as they accept our personality, our values, and what is important to us. Relationships are much better when we feel free to be ourselves around others. Purpose-driven people have good, meaningful, and close relationships. We will encounter fewer problems in intimate relations as well.

SELF-DISCOVERY BRINGS JOY

We go through life handcuffed to a stranger. That stranger is us. This unique stranger spends every day and night with us. The stranger makes many false moves and blunders. The stranger has irrational likes and dislikes. This stranger's moods and impulses are almost impossible to understand.

None of us will make a complete self-discovery. But sometimes in an unpredictable moment, we gather an insight. The created environment or atmosphere is a vital factor. It might be at a retreat center or during a trip to the mountains. Strong environmental forces prevail on us to look inside. The time is usually not when we are content and filled with a happy spirit, or even just after we have been in a joy. The insight comes when we are discouraged or upset or rejected.

We walk along our pathway of life during a bleak period that most of us eventually encounter, a sudden drastic dip in our graph of living, when everything grows stale and flat, energy wanes, and enthusiasm dies.

VISIONS UNVEILED AT A PERSONAL RETREAT

Perhaps we can go on a personal retreat as one Midwestern couple did. A wise old priest told them: Listen carefully.

There were no radios, televisions, music, or even conversations during this retreat. The only sounds they heard were loons singing sad songs. Then the couple listens to the lap of the water from a small lake inside the retreat grounds. They heard a fish jump from the water. A flock of birds waved their wings in flight over their heads. Even the green spring grass appeared to groan as it grew. Everything at the monastery paused, and their racing thoughts stopped. For a moment, when they listened for noises outside themselves, they had to silence their clamorous voices within. Their minds rested in the quietness. The quest contained visions bigger than they were.

The couple went to supper that evening sharing with other searching souls. After the meal, the wise spiritual guide said three words, "Try reaching back." Those words caused them to go where the pain was, in the past. Having gone on retreat before, the couple thought of happy memories of their past. They used the time to recall their times of joy, the wealth of happiness that was half-forgotten. They chose details and recaptured as many as possible. They tried to conceive the joys, to remember and touch up their memories as a painter might retouch the colors or strengthen the outlines of an oil painting of some important event or scene captured and embraced in a moment of time.

They reached back and touched happiness and their videos or paintings of joys that had enriched them and now could be brought back to renew their personalities.

The next morning, hand in hand, exchanging light kisses, they felt even more connected as one. After a light breakfast, their spiritual director acknowledged how bringing back joy brought back a connection to their life mission.

He smiled and gave another word of guidance, "Now re-examine your motives." These words sounded stern. They came not as a gentle suggestion, but as a command.

Both of them took on a defensive stance. They could not figure out anything wrong with their motives. They had traveled to this place to discover themselves as individuals and as a couple. Sure, they wanted to find success. They might even admit that they enjoyed the recognition from others about what a talented, attractive couple they were. Their personalities fit together as pieces in a puzzle. They wanted security. They wanted to find some goals for reaching their dreams.

After a time of prayer, they began to think that perhaps their motives really were not good enough, not in line with their back life purpose. Could this be the reason they were in this spot at that moment in time? They had to really struggle with the suggestion to reexamine their motives. Now they were directed to give something to add to other people's wealth of joy, helping people, making a real contribution. These motives had been lost in their frantic search for a secure life and worldly success. If their motives were wrong, then nothing could be right. When we are concerned only about helping ourselves, taking in our own happiness, we miss our purpose. This direction was the hard core of the retreat. Together they dared to reappraise their lives, to bring their motives into alignment with their capabilities and inner conscience.

It was time to go back home. The baby-spanked pink and blaze of crimson joined the orange and purple streaks in the sky. As they placed their suitcases in the car, they bid goodbye to the old spiritual director. He said one last thing, "As you travel home, be careful, and give your worries to God."

AWARENESS OF WHAT CREATES HAPPINESS

Most of us relate to having a spirit, mind, and a body. We might not understand it or comprehend it, but we believe it. Some believe the whole person becomes what is included in the videos of the mind. So they reason that the mind makes them happy or unhappy. Of course, we realize that the mind and body connection does not lie.

There are repercussions from our negative thinking and actions. Negativity, if held onto, creates unhappy people. We can't hide from the effects of negative thinking.

We are now aware of what creates an atmosphere for happiness. We must be doing some things correctly and we must have given in to our joy instincts or we would not even be as happy as we are. Of course, we all have room for improvement. We can have much more happiness times of joy.

PRACTICAL APPLICATION

Your Personal Joy History:

Describe the happiest time or event in your life.

Name the feelings or experiences you associate with this time and event.

1.

2

3

4

5

6

7.

Describe an unhappy time or event in your life.

Name the feelings associated with this time and event.

1.

2.

3.

4.

5.

6.

7.

8.

9.

10.

What joy killers were in place in your life when this event happened with you?

1.

2.

3.

4.

5.

6.

7.

8.

9.

10.

What did you do to know joy instincts again and how did you overcome this unhappy event or time in your life?

VII

ROADBLOCKS TO JOY

We could never learn to be brave and patient if there were only joy in the world.

— Helen Keller

DIFFERENTIATED PEOPLE WILL FACE ROADBLOCKS on their way to joy. And being imperfect persons, we will continue to discover some holes in the pathway, even some new "tar" as we heal ourselves. After overcoming our denial and going through a re-definition of who we are, we must conquer the most insidious human phase that our problems have produced within us: jealousy. In this name-dropping, label-showing, one-upping world, there is a tremendous freedom in opting out of the race. To live in joy is to choose to run your own race at your own pace with your own reward. Ours is a material world. It's not hard to get into the race to have the most and to envy those running with us.

Jealousy is not one of our emotions, but it involves anger, guilt, fear, and anxiety. Envy is a twin sister of jealousy. Redefining ourselves can help us accept ourselves as we are. It is quite natural to become envious when we are in pain and others—especially our friends—are not. It's easy not to be bitter when we suffer from illness, wondering whether we will die or be constantly rejected or misunderstood. We perceive other people as unburdened, healthy, and without our worries.

JEALOUSY CAN DESTROY US

When our vocation has resulted in failure, when our business or marriage has failed, when we struggle to make ends meet, it's hard not to be jealous of our successful friends. When we have tried to find the perfect love, when we have so wanted family and children and our friends are happily married, it's almost impossible to wish them well. When we have lost loved ones and our acquaintances have not, we are envious.

We permit jealousy to destroy is. We isolate ourselves. We ruin friendships. We break off relationships with family and friends because we cannot be around anyone who knows happiness. We can reason it out. When we are in pain, happy people appear shallow, frivolous, superficial, or phony. We're ringing our hands about ultimate issues. They worry about what kind of new car to purchase. Other people's concerns appear foolish, blind, and selfish. In our valley phases, we would give anything to have such worries. Can we move beyond these jealousies?

We must banish the envy that destroys our lives. Left alone, it will wipe out all our relationships. Unchecked jealousy will leave us with bitterness and anger. We move beyond jealousies by finding the strength to obtain pleasure from other people's joys even when we are in pain and joyless. We must find the wisdom to forgive people for not always being strong enough to face us in our misery. We must excuse and never accuse.

We move beyond our jealousy and envy by remembering that our jealousies and resentments only add to our suffering.

The longer we fail to deal with our envious selves, the longer we will remain in the prisons of our pain.

We are disillusioned to think that we have all the time in the world to change. The average person has 75 years to live, more or less. That's 3,900 Monday mornings to begin again. How many Mondays do we have left? No one really knows for sure.

How many more Mondays to decide to forgive and to ask for forgiveness do we   have left? We say we're just not ready yet. We'll get around to it. But we don't. We waste our precious lifetimes on earth by not forgiving or accepting others' flaws. We can move from envy to compassion. Only when we find the strength to move our muscles will we ever come to understand what returning to life really means.

Of the seven deadly sins, envy is the only one mentioned in the Ten Commandments. "Thou shalt not covet." Envy is the obsessive desire for what someone else has even when we have enough.

We can have a healthy ambition. We can say that we want to improve ourselves. But envy is an unhealthy obsession that we think we must be like another person in order to become fulfilled. We need the attention another is getting. We can be envious of the attention someone else gets at work or in school, or on our sports team. We work hard, but another person gets the credit.

UNSETTLED ROADBLOCK OF ENVY

Envy is a roadblock that keeps us unsettled. We are never content or satisfied. So we cannot enjoy the moment. And joy comes in the moment, a surprise in time. We want something different or better. We just refuse to enjoy the place where we are now. We are like cows grazing over the fence.

Sometimes a new appointment or position of service is a better place. Sometimes transferring to a new school makes much difference to us. But even if we can cross the fence to someplace new, we must remind ourselves that ultimate peace, real contentment, will never come from the things of the world. Our needs are greater than the things we possess.

Some of us end up in debt because of this unsetting feeling that if we just had these things, life would be happy. One product of this roadblock to joy is a low self-esteem. We are just not as good as those who have more. Envy can lead to deep doldrums and depression. It can even lead us to murder as in the story of Cain and Abel.

When we become envious we put others down. If we can't be up there, maybe we can pull them down here. We spread rumors about other people, so their circle of influence will not think that other individuals are all that good.

Moving beyond envy and jealousy requires a softer heart.

We cannot grow hard, indifferent, callous, and unforgiving. We must root out our wishes for friends to fall. Envy roadblocks joy as we are busy pulling others down a few notches.

Our envy causes us to fall. We overcome envy and jealousy by cherishing all that we are, all that we have, and all that we yet will give. We must rejoice in the joy of others even when we lack that joy. We need to take pleasure in others' pleasures wishing them nothing but blessings.

DEPRESSION IS ANOTHER ROADBLOCK TO JOY

Depression takes away one's capacity for joy. Not feeling the negative feelings, the depressed person also has no ability to know the least discussed human emotion, joy. We are emotionally frozen. Nothing will cause us to feel better. With any misfortune or illness, we go get help or wait around for weeks or months until the high calms down or we climb out of the black hole by some miracle. That is, if we're not dead before we find the courage and persistence, trust and faith to move our muscles.

Take life in your own hands and see what happens. It is easier to blame somebody or something for how we are feeling. We might say, "No wonder I am so depressed. Have you seen where I work? Of course, I feel stressed out. The boss is driving me crazy. I just can't cope with these work demands. It causes me to stay in a rage."

We agree that we cannot change where we work, whom we work with, whom we work for, or even the amount of work we do. These are stressors in our lives. But we can change our reactions to them.

Like the little boy who saw a pony under the pile of manure, we can begin to look for positives in our stressors. We cannot change the stressors, but we can change our reactions to them. How are we reacting to the biggest stressors in our lives?

One problem with our inability to experience joy is that we want to be in control. Intense feelings whether positive or negative, are destabilizing.

Souls are made for endurance. We are incredibly well made. In each of us there is a secret part, our deepest ground for being, which has been created for sharing, for heart-to-heart loving relationships and for joy. This freed self is hidden behind unexpressed feelings and dulled imagination, behind our raging anger and hate. The door is closed and we lose all confidence. To endure in life we need a key.

Thoughts are powerful. We are what we think. We have to go through times of depression. We are not bad for being there. We can use our skills of awareness to manage these joyless days. Moving from a reactive to a proactive stance can help. We must take time to prepare ourselves for the next stage.

MAFIA OF THE MIND

Many of us think there is something wrong with us. We have done something wrong. Or worse, we are something wrong. We don't believe we deserve any joy. Subconsciously, we sabotage the joy that could come into our lives. Guilt is the sneakiest and most subtle of the roadblocks to joy. Often we don't feel guilty when we act it. Guilt is the mafia of the mind. Guilt is a condition that separates us from others. Guilt is the extreme opposite of grace. Guilt becomes our moat protecting our personal inner castle. Guilt causes us to destroy our success and our lives. Our inner self cannot reconcile our sudden happiness with our past low self-esteem. We have a choice: to go where the joy is, or to just drop off the deep end.

Guilt is a joy blocker, a mafia of the mind. Guilt becomes a protection plan that we sell ourselves. Thus feeling guilty prepares us for avoidance of anticipated punishment. The problem for us is that this mafia protection involves self-punishment.

Guilt is a masochistic joy blocker. We think that if we punish ourselves enough, then those rude, crude, and indifferent people will take pity on us and not hurt us. We live under the illusion that pain and misery bring redemption rather than innocence. This mafia of our minds causes martyrs to think they are saints. Guilt is a selfish godfather masquerading as God.

There is a religious sect called the Penitentes. They exist among minority fundamentalists, among Muslims and Christians. They practice self-flagellation as a way to find God. Truth is that no matter how much we punish ourselves, guilt is never satisfied until we receive a "good licking" even at our death. This mafia causes us to gloat in our suffering, self-righteously defending our addiction to pain and death. In fact our religious commitment laughs and dances on our grave. Our false faith has proven we are not worthy of joy or even of life itself. After all, we are not perfect, none of us, and guilt shows us what we think we are—dead wrong.

The causes for this job robber are many and they are mutually reinforcing. Some suffer an infant guilt syndrome that is based on another erroneous conclusion that we hurt our mothers at birth. So out of your caring for her, we take on her pain, making a pact with ourselves to suffer so we can protect her from the pain we cause her.

Simultaneously, we can manage to safeguard ourselves from possible retaliation. We suppress our aliveness, our joy, every time we feel intimacy. We close our hearts, our healthy minds, and become uncomfortable, claustrophobic and suffocated and then we explode in our primal rage or leave in our primal terror. This angry explosion and insensible leaving re-enacts the drama of our infant guilt and abandonment. The mafia has sold us separation insurance.

Guilt gives us the idea that we can't live with our life partner or we cannot survive the required intimacy. So the godfather performs a civil ceremony to wed the fear of loss and the fear of love. The godfather and the guilty wedding party smiles as another unsuspecting couple bites the dust.

OUT OF MOTHER'S WOMB

We have forgotten that we are out of mama's womb. The cord has been cut. We are limited by our own minds and our willingness to use a little imagination to transition to joyful living.

We do not hurt our mothers by being born. Her pain resulted from her own birth trauma, her own fear of reliving the intensity of her birth causing her to hold on and to hurt. Under the anesthesia is pain. And under the pain is fear. And under the fear is hurt. But under that hurt is your joy. The only way to heal and get to the joy is to surrender to love and understand that we create our own atmosphere for pain and joy, as everybody else does their own. The tragic guilt at birth is a healthy, loving infant absorbing its loving mother's suffering.

We inherit guilt as a roadblock to joy. The guilt torch is passed on from generation to generation. So if we take on this guilt, this letting of our conscious mind declaring that we are bad, we will tend to gravitate toward punishment. Little children experience disapproval. Parents or social groups such as school, church, or family tradition judge us, criticize us, and evaluate us, just as their parents or culture did them.

Thus the mafia of the mind is cemented into our souls causing us to retreat into ourselves, and we sit and wonder what people will think of us before we act. Guilty people deny their own intuition in favor of pleasing people we think we need to survive.

In fact, we secretly resent these people. And we will blame them for our own patterns of selling ourselves short. Guilt is in search of a villain who will cause us to become helpless victims. Our guilt thinks helplessness is innocence. Original innocence is preferred over original guilt. Joy can neither be created nor destroyed. *Jouissance* is fun and pleasing to the eye. We are surely aware of sensing that children came from heaven and that all of us have an innocent inner child. If we act like devils once in a while, it is only a case of sheep in wolf's clothing. We can begin to overcome this roadblock to our joy as we acknowledge that the innocence in a child's eyes is our own.

There is a wealth of joy for all of us. There is clearly more than enough for everyone to live well. Lack of unconditional love causes a worldwide withholding pattern.

Can you imagine a world not starved for love? Can we create a world free of false guilt or social guilt passed down from generation to generation? Close your eyes. Take a long deep breath. Now imagine our world free of fear and enabled to express ourselves clearly, using all our talents to make affirmative contributions to the well-being of all of us. Close your eyes and enjoy the possible *passionate joy*. Now embrace this vision.

Our brave new world without guilt is a place for self-reliant individuals cooperating rather than competing to make the most of both our internal and external resources.

If our vision appears as a pipe dream, it is because we are so addicted to our illusions of guilt and separation. When can you create an atmosphere for joy and happiness when, in our minds, joy is a paradise lost, an irretrievable womb, a home where we can never go home?

GUILT AND CONSCIENCE

We must forgive ourselves completely. Often we confuse guilt and conscience. Most people listen to the voice of guilt in order to live a life of integrity. Guilt is our mafia disapproving of us. Conscience is our mind reminding us of our real value.

These can be viewed as opposites. Our ego can confuse us into thoughts that we are people of the "guilty conscience."

Our conscience is not guilty. Conscience is our voice of wisdom that drives our guilt up and out of us, restoring us to give innocence its natural throne.

Guilt is a part of our self-disapproval. The antidote is a heavy dose of self-love and forgiveness. We can feel guilty about failing or succeeding, judging or hurting, sometimes about even existing. The remedy is to accept all these aspects of ourselves and stop using them to demonstrate our culture's primal laws.

SUBDUING OUR GUILT

Conquering the roadblock of jealousy requires that we love and forgive other people. Subduing guilt means to love and forgive ourselves.

Some of our guilt is real. Tragedy brings guilt. We should have made another choice. We could have done more. These are refrains rushing through us. Guilt enters when our addictions or illnesses tear our families apart. Guilt results from adultery that destroys trust, deceit, betrayal, cruelty, bringing pain to people we care about and love. Guilt is good for us in that we are aware so we can correct a wrong. People who feel no guilt frighten us. Healthy guilt helps us to learn remorse and it reminds us to behave differently in the future. Excessive guilt is a misuse of our energy. Do we choose to spend the times of our lives improving ourselves or do we spend the rest of our lives berating ourselves.

Guilt comes when someone close to us dies before we can repair our relationship with them. Guilt brings blame for our procrastination, for our not having enough emotional strength to speak the words we need to say, or for lacking the capacity to forgive when we still had the opportunity.

How can we subdue this mafia of our minds? We hold on to guilt because it enables us to survive. We think being guilty is a way to retain our sanity in the face of life's insanity. Guilt creates in our dysfunctional thinking order from the chaos. Guilt enables us to think of a tragedy as not just senseless or haphazard, but that everything has a purpose. Our mind's mafia tells us that we are the cause. Guilt allows us to feel that we are powerful despite tragedy that has left us feeling helpless and small. We are so powerful that we can hold ourselves responsible for events that were out of our control.

FALSE GUILT

How long will we continue to punish ourselves for circumstances we did not cause? Life without groundless guilt frees up our souls to renew the joy. Subduing guilt means to forgive ourselves for not being the person we fantasized we could be. Lightening our load brings peace for the next situation and ending our suffering that began when our tragedy struck us. Only then can we again feel the joy. We can begin to understand that we deserve fun once again. And finally, we can stop fearing God and start approaching our Higher Power with love, even in protest, in sadness, in longing, in joy.

The word sin comes from the Greek language. It means "missing the mark." There are many Hebrew words for sin also. Now can you imagine how different our childhoods would have been if we were told, *When we sin we simply miss the mark of being the best we could be*? Any of us who heard that would have a different perspective on our behavior and its ramifications.

Perception is everything when it comes to experiencing guilt. Only then can we acknowledge the irrationality of most guilt or false guilt feelings. Let us not die while we are still living.

THERE SHALL BE NO REGRETS

Nothing in life is more exciting and rewarding than the sudden flash of insight that leaves us as changed persons. That change is always for the better. Such moments are as rare as a joy experience. Sometimes the insight comes from the word of action of a friend. Sometimes it arrives as insight from an enemy, one of those people who appear forever as rude, crude, and indifferent.

We have heard that little term many times. "If only" we had done something different. "If only" we didn't have to live with this disability. "If only" we had been brought up on another rung of the economic ladder, we would be happy. "If only" we had had some other person's experiences, advantages, or gifts. "If only" my temperament was different. "If only" I was not so selfish or so uncontrollable.

An old professor at Vanderbilt used to tell his students, "If you would just stop saying 'if only,' you'd get somewhere." Smoking on his Scottish pipe, he'd tell students, "The trouble with living by your 'if only' outlook is that it never changes your life one bit. You keep looking to the past. You can't change the past. 'If only' thinking ruins your present and will do nothing for your future."

Our plans don't always work out. Maybe for years they never did come out like we had planned. Perhaps we made some mistakes. We fell for charm or deceit or temptation or some illusive dream. Every one of us missed the mark in these and a hundred other human ways. Mistakes are what we learn from. But, if we lament them or keep on regretting them, insist on talking about them, we are not learning from them.

Some of us never get out of the past tense. If we're not careful, we'll regret even being alive. That perverse streak of dwelling in the past is a roadblock to our joy. Hashing over old valley times that we now regret will just keep us there. Some of us actually enjoy seeing those old videos in our mind day after day. Nothing new and refreshing can get in our stubborn ole television of the mind screens. And, if we are truthful, we actually enjoy it. Perhaps we have permitted ourselves to be addicted to the misery. Maybe we sort of enjoy being the main character in those old movies.

We need to shift the focus. There shall be no regrets. Why not use another phrase? Instead of continuing with "if only," fill your mind with the words, "next time."

When we say "next time" there is hope for us. We'll be aware of our regret and the old films will continue to sit on our shelves of our life experiences. Only now there is hope. Only now will we learn from life. We will push away the roadblock of regret from our happiness highways. Journaling our daily life experiences can enable us to see our pattern. Reading back can be therapeutic as we accept everything that has happened to us with no regrets.

The repeating national champion University of Southern California football team uses passing by outstanding quarterbacks in their offense. During a practice session, the quarterback threw several blanks. He threw a weak ball that resulted in an interception. He threw another pass so long nobody could catch it. Then he said, "If only I had had more control." The coach said, "Next time throw sooner." The wide receiver said, "Next time, I'll run faster." They did and perhaps it's the Oklahoma team that now expresses its regrets. And the joyous beat goes on, "Fight on, for USC."

PRACTICAL APPLICATION

What were your roadblocks to passionate joy?

1.

2.

3.

4.

5.

6.

7.

8.

9.

10.

How did you overcome them?

Who helped you along the way?

Reflect on this prayer for joys and concerns:

Spirit of life and spirit of grace,
Rest with us this day, in this place.
We lift up every joy, every gladness,
We hold up every hurt, every sadness
Spoken in this good company
As well as every secret feeling
Held quiet in the hollows of our hearts.

VIII

DOING WHAT YOU HAVE POWER TO DO

The sharing of joy, whether physical, emotional, psychic, or intellectual, forms a bridge between the sharers which can be the basis for understanding much of what is not shared between them, and lessons the threat of their difference.

— Audre Lorde

DOING WHAT WE HAVE THE power to do means doing what we are. We want to live energetically and productively. But to be happy and to enjoy life, we need to make our living by doing work that we want to do. We need to make a point to find some enjoyment out of our work each day. If we cannot "go where the joy is," then we need to change our work. It is important that we like what we are doing. Of course, not every minute of any work has continuous joy. Personal fulfillment is our key, not just making money. Deep personal satisfaction is an ever-present source of personal strength and sustenance that benefits you and others around you.

STEPS TO DOING WHAT YOU WANT TO DO

How can we manage to do what we want to do? How can we use ourselves more effectively and enjoy the days we are given to add value to our world? Setting our sights is essential. We need a personal vision.

Decide what you want to do most of all. Then we plan and work to achieve our objective. Carl Jung said, "Man invented rulers out of sheer laziness."

We can decide to rule ourselves. Fellow kings, go for it! We can guide our destiny instead of yielding to whatever comes along. Working toward your wanted goal might be to zigzag toward it, sometimes working at jobs outside of your vision, but never forgetting where the joy is. If we are to pursue our most gratifying individual mission, instead of being ruled by others or to be oppressed by a job that you abhor, you must exert much courage and effort.

HAPPINESS MEANS MORE THAN MONEY

To be happy, we might receive little recognition and small amounts of money. Would we still choose to do what we are doing if there were no such thing as money? Would we continue to do our work just because we are driven to do it? Of course, each of us has a personal vision of the world and an inner compulsion to present it to others, to bring creative order out of chaos.

In determining and setting our goals, we must realize that no matter how we organize and change our way of life for the better, we will not achieve what we want unless we change ourselves for the better. If we don't do that self-evaluation daily, we might be like the man who finally got a new job. He said, "My job is far more desirable than my work used to be. Trouble is I am still what I used to be. I continue to be unsure of myself and depressed about it."

To find joy in work our deciding factor must not be what others think you should do, but what we think, and even more do what we are not what somebody else is. Beware of making the wrong analysis. It is important that we don't misdirect our thinking so that we come up with the wrong direction, because we reacted against something rather than going toward a more joyous way. Self-fulfillment is always important for knowing happiness and those moments of joy. Not always just dreaming about what we yearn for and need, but doing something constructive. We can make more joyous life happen to us. And we are the prime beneficiaries. The greatest use of life is to spend it for something that will outlast it.

LIVING IN JOY FOR A LONG TIME

We have the power to live well for a long time. Do you have dreams for the next fifty years? What about twenty-five years? Or even five years?

We know that if we only have a morning project, at noon when we finish the job, we'll be tired and bored. We'll probably waste the rest of the day. But if we have scheduled something to do in the morning, something else to do in the afternoon, and another thing to do in the evening, our minds and bodies will keep humming all day. We'll have purpose all day and sparkle in our moving of our mind and body muscles.

If we don't have projects to do after we are sixty or seventy, we must be planning to die at that age. When you finish them, you'll be "done," and from then on you'll just coast along. Don't die before you die.

Stretch out your expectations. Plan years down the road. With modern medicine and a good lifestyle, many of us will live past 100 years of age. George Burns said, "You can't help getting older, but you don't have to get old." Be happy if you live many years. After all, as Pablo Picasso said when he was 86, "It takes a long time to become young."

Some life factors needed to live a long time include: a positive mindset, realism,

good work habits, moderate eating habits, good physical health, reduced stress and anxiety, optimism, good marital and social relationships, and a good heredity.

We must pace ourselves to last long enough to accomplish the goals. Some of us burn out at forty. Some race through life at breakneck speed and by sixty-five are finished. Some do it literally—and finish even sooner. The government doesn't send Social Security checks to graveyards. People who drive themselves like they have no tomorrow might not have a tomorrow. Life is not a forty-yard dash. It's a long run.

Stretching out our goals and pacing ourselves to achieve them will keep us busy.

We must find our life's purpose, choose creative work designed just for us, and never quit.

Did you ever notice that people in many kinds of occupations burn out, but not artists? Symphony conductors, writers, poets, and musicians function well into their 90s and beyond. Punching a clock and endless holes in metal on a factory assembly line or in a boring government job appears to atrophy minds and spirits. Creative work, maybe even designing new shapes or sizes for that metal, stimulates the mind and spirit.

Every high school graduate should be required to write a poem, play a musical instrument, or create something out of wood or clay. Otherwise, we dry up. We burn out. We rust out.

NEVER RETIRE FROM LIFE

We need to keep our juices flowing. Learn something new even if you are 92. If you are working in a dull, static place, there is something that needs improving. Can you get your mind going? Can you create or help find a new way of doing the work?

Never quitting does not mean never retire from your present job or vocation. Never retire to an unworthy purpose. An Omaha, Nebraska, insurance company reported that the average retiree receives only ten monthly retirement checks. When many people quit working, they quit living.

Puttering is not enough. We need something important and worthy to do, even if it's volunteer work. Retirees all over the world volunteer to be involved in other people's lives. They are not only deeply appreciated, but they have a ball. So be useful. Forget yourself. Be full of whatever you are doing. To guard your loves and relationships and your reputation throughout your years, to be adored rather than to get obnoxious, you must choose to serve rather than to be served.

JOY AND OUR PLAYFUL WORLD

We do not stop playing because we grow old. We grow old because we stop playing. Nothing is childish. When older people know they have permission to play, they reduce their inhibitions and enjoy themselves. It really feels good when a ten-year-old knocks on your door and says, "Can grandpa come out and play today?" Stay tuned into your inner child and you will keep having fun.

Play is an antidote for workaholics. Bumblebees are

workaholics. They don't know when to stop. They literally work themselves to death. A typical bumblebee wears itself out in three to six weeks. Young bumblebees begin working at an earlier age than do honeybees. Bumblebees start their career at 48 hours, two days of age. Honeybees start their careers at two weeks. Bumblebees put in more hours. Bumblebees are out working while honeybees are still sleeping in. Sometimes, if the night is clear, bumblebees work the whole night through. Workaholic traps easily become habits. Being a workaholic appears so commendable. Some people look at over-workers with admiration and approval. They always stay late just "to finish up a few things" or "to clean off my desk." Management rewards the workaholic in a performance appraisal that stresses the doing "beyond and above" the requirements and working hours. The size of the briefcase that goes home over the weekend indicates loyalty to the organization.

What price do we pay for those extra hours of work? The price is measured in losing relationships, failing health, and the high risk of an early death. Few people on their deathbeds wish that they had given more time to their job. They wish they had spent more time loving and living.

We are human beings not human doings. For a honeybee, being means admiring the flowers it visits, enjoying the sun on its wings, tasting the honey. Take time for each moment in your lifetime.

Reports of joy experiences in older people all contain a sense of being born again. They believe they have found their internal fountain of youth. Whenever people appear much younger than their years, the reason is less their physical appearance than the ageless joy with which they approach life.

We can understand this as we observe a grandpa or grandma when they greet a grandchild. Watch the years peel away. Being born again does not necessarily imply a religious change, but something seems to happen with our joy responses that revive our spirits.

Joy not only causes us to feel younger, but behaving younger makes you have more joy times. Bake some cookies with your grandkids. Pitch a ball. Play a game. You'll be happier just by playing. Now don't play like an adult. We ruin everything that way. Allow yourself just to play in the service of your joy.

One characteristic of joy is an indescribable experience of understanding the world beyond daily stressors and survival. Joy gives a deeper appreciation, even a sense of amazement at all the times of our lives and our connection to others.

SERVING AND LIVING

Never take service for granted. As long as we live, we will appreciate it, say thanks, and encourage those who serve. We must continue to wait on others. Tend to use each day "to make somebody else enjoy life." If our lives are lived to help others, we'll want to live a long time, and chances are, we will.

For example, should you decide between a career in art and business management? Ask yourself, what is my objective? What rewards do you desire? What will give more personal fulfillment? There is no right or wrong. Go where the joy is.

And going for it means a willingness to accept responsibility for bad as well as good results. Personal choice means personal responsibility. Otherwise another failure can cause us to fall apart and we will be unhappier than before.

What do you think are your talents? Are you using them in your passionate work now? If you could have ten other career choices, what would they be? Who would you be? What was one of your real moments of success? What really happened before that photo or national news article was taken? What events led up to your winning that award?

Joseph Campbell wrote about "following your bliss." What does he mean? What is your bliss, your passion? What activity makes you glow? What puts you into a timeless flow?

When we were little children, we got report cards filled out by teachers to tell our parents how we were doing in school. It is difficult to transition ourselves from external judgment to internal acceptance. This journey is one we must make to reach our essential selves.

SUCCESS IS AN INSIDE JOB

Real success is internal. Most of the time, nobody else is aware that we have reached it. Success is being aware that we can do it. We have gone for it. And is it not a comfort to know this awareness and internalizing of it can never be taken away.

When we find success, we don't have to compare ourselves to others. The force of jealousy diminishes. With real success, we want others to have the same opportunities that we have had, to do what they would love to do themselves. We become generous of spirit.

Young mothers with responsibilities outside their homes have terrible pulls between their jobs and their children. We are all human. Even those mothers, and fathers, who appear that they can do everything well, find an enmity between daily life and work life.

To enjoy real success, we have to be who we are. A pastor of a rural church in Nebraska gave his first sermon to his new congregation. He led off by telling a joke. Nobody laughed. He was a local pastor who had no seminary training. He had heard ministers start sermons with jokes. Nothing is worse than a joke that falls flat, or one that is not understood. He was embarrassed and frustrated. His experience taught him that being a comedian was not his style. He was better at just presenting his story naturally. If any humor happened to pop up, that was just fine. He had to be himself.

We all have unique styles. Have you discovered yours? Did somebody help you in that quest to your personal truth? When was that first time that you looked at yourself in the mirror and thought, "Now you, dear me, I do enjoy! This is more like it."

The inescapable and brutal fact of living is that if we aim to fulfill ourselves through pursuing our own personal concepts, then we must handle difficulties and failures. We might succeed. Or we might fail totally as far as outer environment recognition and approval are concerned, without failing within ourselves. That is possible if we accept responsibility at the start of our stage of life and throughout our years. Otherwise, we are tempted to strike out irrationally at others to evade our responsibility and imperfections. Going where the joy is comes not from escaping and evading our responsibilities but in facing up to them. Turtles make progress only when they stick their necks out.

When we were born, we cried, and our world rejoiced. We must live our lives so that when we die, the world cries and we rejoice. So goes an ancient saying. How do we allow ourselves to be open so that others rejoice in us? One simple answer is that we have vision for our lives that is so big our own lives are not enough to sustain the vision.

For us to "go for it" we need a goal so great that we have to move past the perimeter of personal pleasure, beyond the border of me and mine. "Going where the joy is" means canning our can'ts, and moving toward others. Most of us are used to looking no farther than the ends of our own noses. Even when we think we are looking out for the rest of us or even the "least of us," often the focus is still on us.

Many of us recall the story of a man going shopping with his four-year-old child in the cart seat. That little boy was a terror. He was reaching for things on the shelves. He whined and screamed at the top of his lungs. But the man was heard calmly saying, "It will be all right son. Just be quiet and be calm, John. John, now just settle down."

But the child in the shopping cart seat continued to make a nuisance. Finally, a woman had had enough. She walked over to the man, pointed to his kid, and said, "Why don't you do something with John and get him under control?"

The man answered, "That's not John. That's Jake. I'm John." Even if we appear to be focused on others, we remain the center of our attention.

We have been conditioned to think and speak with singular personal pronouns. Many books are written that way. "Me" and "mine" insist on getting into every communication. We are much like two English characters that lived back in the 1800s.

An English newspaper carried a story about two men, James Whistler and Oscar Wilde. The short note said they spent the day talking about themselves as they usually did daily in a pub near Brighton. Whistler clipped the little article and sent it to his friend Wilde. He wrote a comment on the clipping: "I wish these reporters would be more accurate. If you recall, Oscar, we were talking about me." Wilde replied by telegram: "It is true that we were talking about you, but I was thinking about me."

We are self-focused people living in a world with others. During a class at Vanderbilt University, John Killinger told about a psychologist who conducted a survey of beliefs and attitudes of college-age youth. He learned that almost all of the late teens and young twenty-year-olds interviewed expressed a desire for greatness and satisfaction.

However, none of them saw a connection between greatness in themselves and service to others. The psychologist concluded: "They are a generation accustomed to being served, not to serving."

All of life is not about us. We are but a grain of sand on a beach. Those who think life is only about them will end this life with neither the world crying nor themselves rejoicing. Our individual lives are not interesting enough or challenging enough to sustain any of us for a lifetime. The self-focused person quickly becomes bored with self and gets disappointed when having to deal with a valley time.

Happiness comes, as do moments of joy, when we bring other people and their needs within the range of our concern and as we give ourselves to them. Steven Covey said, "Service to others is the rent we pay for the privilege of living in this world."

Russian poet Yevgeny Yevtushenko said, "Do not be afraid when you suffer, forget the vulgar, insulting fairy tale that has been hammered into your heads since childhood that the meaning of life is to be happy. The only true happiness is to share in the sufferings of the unhappy."

During the past few decades, parents in the United States have taught their children to value material prosperity above all else. There is more to joy in life than having things. Contrary to what the bumper sticker claims, whoever dies with the most toys does not win. Our children need to learn what really counts. *Jouissance* is the excessive joy experience that enables us to understand lasting meaning and to learn what cannot be taken by life's uncertainties or by death's certainty. Our children need to learn about the joy that can be fund by entering into another's suffering and pain.

Mother Teresa, who gave her life to helping the poor in India by enabling them to die with dignity and love, knew the internal joy. She shifted her concern exclusively from self to include others, and in so doing, incurred a loss of personal pleasure. Why? Because she was who we are all supposed to be. We can "can" our can'ts.

Keep all your channels open. Your energy will be translated into action. We cannot fully understand the mystery of the life of human energy. All we can do is to remain open to it, to clear a way for it, and then let it move through us. We must make room for serendipity experiences, new thoughts, new ideas, new people, new appreciation for those already in your life and those who drop into it in moments of surprise.

POWERFUL VICTIMS

All Rosa Parks was doing was trying to get home from work. But she stumbled into becoming the symbol of the Civil Rights movement by refusing to go to the back of the bus. The powerful impact of her unplanned action has resonated for her, and for us all, ever since that day in Birmingham. Many reflected on her passionate joy at her funeral.

Victims seem to be powerless. They might even think of themselves as powerless. Those who are ill mentally or physically, minorities, and older people are able to receive much attention from the rest of us. Victims learn how to exploit their so-called hopeless conditions. They are not helpless in getting other people involved in solving their problems. Part of life's purpose for some of us is to rescue them from their struggles.

Persecutors of life's victims are filled with insecurity and anxiety, fear, and guilt. As persecutors, we might appear extremely secure and confident. Sometimes traditional morality and righteousness are on our side. Words they use are should, must, have to, or ought. We might attack the victim for being weak, doing things inadequately, which means not doing things most of us see as the correct way. Remember it is the characteristic of joy to come in the mourning.

ACCEPTANCE IS THE HIGHEST FORM OF FAITH

Doing what we have the power to do involves acceptance. That truth is rejected by people who refuse to admit limitations. They hide behind excuses and labels, stigmas and half-truths. They respond to the hard times of life by anger and bitterness. Repairing damaged relationships or a broken life requires acceptance of some thorny and difficult reality that must be faced, or we'll have no power at all.

This truth is like a bright color of thread running through a whole tapestry. We understand this, for example, when we deal with alcoholism. It is such a mysterious and grim disease. Recovery begins by accepting the unacceptable. It begins in a damp church basement when we finally accept the words by which we introduce ourselves at an Alcoholics Anonymous meeting, "I am an alcoholic."

In the beginning those words are so difficult, hideously hard to say. But in terms of courage, joy, and ultimate happiness, the rewards are beyond measure.

We confuse acceptance with apathy. They are as different as night and day, darkness and lightness. Apathetic people fail to distinguish between what can and what cannot be helped. Acceptance makes that distinction. Our will to effort is not brought forth in apathy. Acceptance frees us of unreasonable expectations and impossible burdens. Accept, forgive, and move on.

Life is full of hills and valleys. Nothing is as we think it ought to be. We are never as strong or good as we would like to be. With each sunrise, there comes the gift of a new day. Each day gives us a new beginning, new opportunities, and new challenges. Reinhold Niebuhr's famous prayer can be read as, "Lord, grant me the strength to change things that need changing, the courage to accept things that cannot be changed, and the wisdom to know the difference."

OUR POWER FOR THOSE VALLEY DAYS

Those bad days when we exist through each day can be devastating. Most bad days are predictable. We're in pain. Some might have just lost a job, received a divorce notice, lost a loved one, or we might have been told our health is to the point of possible death.

There is nothing we can do to change the fact. Say a prayer, decide to be bold, and gather all the power you have left and get through it. You have the power to relieve your bad days. You might not see instant relief, but you have taken a positive proactive step. Some of the pain might go away temporarily, but you can be in a better frame of mind.

Getting outside, out in a natural surrounding can help. Skipping like a child through a park or garden can help you recall some joys of your past. Even if you feel that you hate another person for how they wounded you, you can focus on any good days. Surely if you were married for twenty years, something good happened. Some of your good days might have been while outdoors. If you feel you can't get outside, open a window to get some fresh air. Watching children laugh and play, catching a glimpse of lovers walking around, or seeing another wounded soul moving the muscles despite the pain can help us get focused and motivated to make an effort.

Friends help. Companionship and a distraction from your routine have the potential to be more powerful than any medication. Ask somebody to come see you. Helen Keller reminded us, "Alone we can do so little; together we can do so much." Perhaps you can drive off to the mountains, or to a beach, or just drive to the woods. This activity with another will give you a break. You need to be refreshed during bad days. Even a short walk down the street with an understanding friend can help. Exercise helps us maintain our health.

Water is healing. Take a nice bath with some relaxing crèmes or colored water that relaxes your body. If you have one, go to the jacuzzi, or take time to go enjoy one at a motel. Swimming in water can help. If you can't swim or are afraid of water, just wade in a creek, skip rocks across the water, or momentarily float your bad days away on a raft or lay in shallow water.

Enjoy a massage. Some people swear by them. You have the power to take a hot shower. Keep clean on good or bad days. Hypnosis or guided imagery can help. Biofeedback is often a possibility. Yoga, playing a game that you enjoyed in childhood, or the activity of just watching others, can become life enablers on painful days.

Pet therapy has been a healing source for ages. Hang out with some animals. Some animals, cats and dogs and horses, have been trained to help us on bad days. Animals not only offer entertainment, but they give distraction from our suffering. Pets promote social interaction. They relive stress and they motivate physical movement and exercise.

Rent a comical movie. Laughter is another proven help on valley days. Laughter reduces pain and suffering. That's something you always have the power to do. Laughing triggers the release of endorphins. Norman Cousins is a famous example of this laughter therapy. He used funny movies like Marx brothers and the old Candid Camera videos to help him through his valley days of suffering from ankylosing spondylitis, a disease of the connecting tissues of the spine. His belly laughter helped give him some pain-free sleep.

Do what you have the power to do. Research and experiment and you'll discover something that will help. Trust your instincts. Go for it with you intuition. Experts might not know what fits you when you are in a fit. Explore your options. Pain and suffering, those valley days are not welcomed guests that are determined not to depart.

Endorse yourself for making an effort. Stretch your muscles. You're not designed to just sit. Wear nylons in cold weather to keep your legs warm. Stiff limbs don't care to move. Buy yourself a good mattress. After all we sleep away one third of our lives. Bad sleep just adds more misery to bad days. Some who suffer restless leg syndrome use a body pillow between their legs when sleeping. Body pillows can help anyone stay comfortable through the night.

A healthy mind is the key to getting through bad days. Adjusting our focus will heal or minds even if our bodies fail us. Acceptance of bad days helps our attitudes. Suffering and pain can be roadways to positive change. Bad days enable us to redefine who we are. Values and priorities get in order during the days we have to spend in our valley times. Remind yourself of your powerful brain. Do what you have the power to do. Trust your relationship to your Higher Power. The bad days can give us freshness about our human identity, a newfound spirituality. Thomas Edison said, "If we all did the things we are capable of doing, we would literally astound ourselves."

PRACTICAL APPLICATION

List ways you can cultivate joy instinct creators that are presently lacking in your life.

1.

2.

3.

4.

Develop your personal plan for experiencing joy when times are tough. Establishing a joy instinct strategy can create an atmosphere where joy and miracles will happen in your life making it easier to stay grounded when things are not going well. Describe your plan in detail.

IX

SEXUALITY AND JOY

She turned now and started kissing me with such a hungry agony that my burnt shoulders began to throb until tears came into my eyes.

"Ah!" she said softly and sadly. "You are crying."

"I wish I could. I have lost the knack."

— Lawrence Durrell

A BEAUTIFUL WOMAN ONCE SAID, "Love is a feeling. Sex is a sport." Neither is true. Like the woman described in Proverbs 7:6-23, she had effective means of persuasion to seduce her targeted men. I wonder what her quality of life is now.

People play with fire when it comes to sex. Sex is not a sport with no rules. Sex is not a feeling for when the feelings are gone, the relationship ends with two or more people deeply hurt.

Sexuality was a positive gift for the Hebrew people and for people in the universe. From the beginning of life, human beings were acquainted with the erotic energy within.

Childhood is not a time of sexual dormancy. From birth, babies are capable of sexual arousal. Children delight in their curiosity about the body's sensations and exploration of its nooks and crannies, its openings, its operations. Humans find pleasure in the heart, in times of joy, and even in their tears as the erotic potential of the universe pulsates through the body.

God is present when bonded partners share intercourse. Many believe that God shows favor or disfavor by opening or closing the womb.

The most lavish source of insight into human nature lies in the sexual personality. Sexual attitudes, activities, and fantasies constitute the most graphic measure we have of character. In sexuality, we express basic relations with ourselves and others.

Sometimes our original erotic potential is judged as immodest, immoral, or impure by parents and teachers and religious leaders in their words and actions. For those touched affectionately by their parents, touch is seldom extended beyond childhood. As we grow out of the cute stage, parents become uncomfortable with our developing bodies and most touching stopped. So we became convinced that something was wrong with our bodies.

We observed and touched ourselves with our growing breasts, public hair, and the genital sensations that made us untouchable to our parents. Of course, parents were trying to act in the correct way stirring miles away from the incestuous behavior of evil parents or relatives. So child and parent and the way society views sexuality compounded the growing discomfort and anxiousness in the family.

During the days of adolescence, the vagina replaces the clitoris as the focus of sexual pleasure and society reduces sexuality to genital intercourse. Sexuality in its raw definition required a partner. Most early body knowing and erotic autonomy were not cultivated by parents, so young people became ignorant of the mechanics of sex. They depended on others to learn about the wonders of our bodies and the erotic potential and the capacity for sensual delight. By college, or even high school days people take responsibility for their own sexual pleasure and satisfaction.

God would have us to grow in love with our bodies as we discover what arouses us and understand our sexual wounds and armoring, and we can deepen in satisfaction and contentment with ourselves. Churches and schools and communities can teach about the beauty of the gift of sex as an essential prerequisite to sharing healthy sexual intimacy with a beloved partner.

Harry Hollis expresses some helpful thoughts that have been shared in many church groups:

> Lord, it's hard to know what sex really is.
> Is it some demon put here to torment me?
> Or some delicious seducer from reality?
> It is neither of these, Lord.
>
> I know what sex is. It is body and spirit.
> It is passion and tenderness. It is strong
> embrace and gentle handholding.
> It is open nakedness and hidden mystery.
> It is joyful tears on honeymoon faces, and
> it is tears on wrinkled faces at a golden
> wedding anniversary.
>
> Sex is a quiet look across the room, a love note
> on a pillow, a rose laid on a breakfast plate,
> laughter in the night.
>
> Sex is life, not all of life, but wrapped up
> in the meaning of life.
>
> Sex is your good gift, O God, to enrich life,
> to continue the race, to communicate, to show
> me who I am, to reveal my mate, to cleanse through
> one flesh.

Lord, some people say sex and religion don't mix.
But your Word says sex is good. Help me to keep
it good in my life. Help me to be open about sex,
and still protect its mystery. Help me to see that
sex is neither demon or deity. Help me not to climb
into a fantasy world of imaginary sexual partners.
Keep me in the real world to love the people you have created.

Teach me that my soul does not have to frown at sex
for me to be a Christian. It is hard for many people to say,
"Thank God for sex." They need to know that sex and
gospel can be linked together again. They need to hear the
Good News about sex. Show me how I can help them.
Thank you, Lord, for making me a sexual being.
Thank you for showing me how to treat others
with trust and love. Thank you for letting me talk
to you about sex. Thank you that I feel free to say,
"Thank God for sex."

What better place to celebrate human sexuality than church? In some joyous days of the history of Christianity, some have presented their religion as an anti-sexual community.

Why are we not free to celebrate one of the most important gifts in all human life in the local church? Why do we not take the responsibility for sex education and attitudes about sexuality in youth retreats, family life conferences, and in the preaching of our worship?

SEXUALITY AND RELATIONSHIPS

In marital therapy, sexuality is the number one hang-up in relationships. Failure to embrace the gift of sexuality prevents happiness and joy in relationships. The desperate need is to deal with the emotions that come from living life. Sexuality is the most natural part of our existence.

We have heard of so much distortion and trouble talking about this gift from God. The vagina and penis are vital parts of the body like the eye or the ear.

Our bodies are related to our souls and our emotions. We cannot abuse our bodies without abusing our emotions and our visionquests for moments or joy.

Christian love will not cover up problems with play acting, but a community of love exposes our difficulties and valleys in life in the open where they can be dealt with realistically and honestly.

Four simple questions in pastoral psychotherapy sessions reveal much of the concerns of couples: Are you happily married? Does your spouse love you? What do you think about her or him? How do you feel when thinking of your partner?

The answers depend on their experience in the area of sexual acceptance and wisdom, and their experiences of being secure, protected, and appreciated.

God is just as fascinated by our sexual lives as God is with our prayer lives. He is disappointed as we are when our sex lives yield no times of joy or happiness. God's delight is there when we are in a joy in sexuality, using the divine gift to delight each other and to glorify our creator by becoming human beings that are fully alive.

Every experience in human sexuality will not put us in a joy experience. We set ourselves up for failure if that is our expectation. Of course, sometimes sex is awkward. It may be unsatisfying for newly weds with no experience in having intercourse. Sex is fun as its mechanics and sensuality are learned. We are human beings, not machines. Sexuality at its best is a spiritual communication. It is not just a feeling or a sport.

Take responsibility for your own sexual pleasure. Sex is not something you just do for or to another person.

By observing how we think, dream, and act when we enjoy our lives, we can find out who we are and what be believe. People with graceful and appealing sexual lives enter it with prayer and meditation. It can be the most holy time of our being.

There is a connectedness between our sexuality and our faith. The rite of initiation into Jewish faith is circumcision, the dedication of the male organ by sacrificing part of it. For the male it was the most sacred and holy part of his body. This enabled him to continue God's mission on earth.

Sex is a gift to give pleasure. In very rare moments it gives us joy. Perhaps it was a joy for you, perhaps long ago, at your first orgasm. Perhaps you sensed contentment after having sex with your loved one after contradictions about some problem finally stilled in your head.

Most wives and husbands or partners do not know the other's sexual sensation development. Women usually have a slower rhythm than men. Delicate consideration is needed. Happiness in a sex life comes from within as much as from without. Sex brings pleasure and affirmation to those whose souls have created an atmosphere for happiness and joy times.

Experiencing life in that precious moment of sexual climax is to share God's gift. Few experiences are more spiritually more meaningful than human beings expressing love through sex and that sexual time within the perfect will of God.

All that is basic to our souls is expressed through sexual choices. Sexuality is what a person is in the depths of personal being. The way we have sex and with whom, is just as much our choice as where we vacation, how we spend our money, or where we get our spirituality.

SEXUALITY MEANS MANY THINGS

Sex is what the soul and mind conceives: a time of joy, a means of procreation, a sport, a worthless experience, a valued escapade, an evil, a good gift, a communion with God, a source of self-esteem, a road to peace, a retreat from loneliness, an ideal state of being, a luxury, a way to rebel, a route to freedom, a death wish, a cause, a form of communication, a way to show affection, an escape, a reward, euphoria, an art, love, beauty, faith, an instrument of aggression, a tool for anger, a duty, a submission, ecstasy, whimsy, a mode of exploring, a skill, a sign of good health, a rite of passage, a biological function, a pleasure, a sensory experience.

Sexual problems relate to the wellsprings of other life difficulties. Nobody reaches their potential. Uncertainties and confusion and our missing the mark in life plague us all. Sexual revolutions caused confused, uncommitted, frustrated persons to take on its simplistic, hedonistic identities. Sexual journalism and pornography lied to us by just labeling sexual personality as cold or hot, inhibited or liberated. Some need healing of the soul to become sexually fulfilled. Sex is a part of the total personality and may require forgiveness and acceptance. Nobody can create a new sexual past. Sex blooms within the heightened form of commitment.

Happiness looks like a love connected relationship. Lovers relax as they hold each other in sleep. If you have ever made love and then had to separate from your loved one before intimacy needs were satisfied, you know how it feels. Your very soul lacks being fulfilled.

Men and women spend their lives complaining about inner sexual deadness. They try hard to gain attention. Anything. Anything for the love they never perceived in their childhood or youthful years. Anything for the love their manipulations can never achieve.

Some questions to consider: What emotional need causes you to be aroused to sex? Do you want sex when you are lonely or feel isolated or feel unloved? Is sex giving you reassurance? Do you tend to routinize sex but having it on Tuesday and Saturday only at the same time and place?

One foundation for a kind of sexual schizophrenia is created when people consider sex as a function like breathing or eating. Sexuality or intercourse is really not vital to life or committed love. We do not have sex because we need it. We have sex because it is something we want and it is a part of our covenant in relationships.

Women and men can be taught that they need not put on a show of emotions, a wild and sensuous display of color, or words that claim superior words of seductive power, such as "Nobody else can love you like I can," just to get attention. A committed person knows they'll be loved even if the woman was a brown wren girl wet-feathered in the rains of life and the man is ordinary. Committed partners are not interested in each other as ornaments. They attract powerful men and women as visionary partners, friends, and lovers.

Sex is not a feeling and it is not just a sport. Sexuality is your birthright as a creature from God. And with this gift you can be assured that there will be moments of joy.

PRACTICAL APPLICATION

Create a sacred place for sexuality. Take care of your body with exercise, smells, flowers, or candles.

Fill the space with affirming music and images.

Bless the parts of your body that have been difficult to acknowledge. Pay attention to these areas: scars, a place trespassed by another, a layer of fat, attend discomfort without judgment. Say to yourself, "My body is good. It is created for pleasure and delight I am blessed."

X

JOY, LOVE, AND FRIENDSHIP

We choose our joys and sorrows long before we experience them.

— Khalil Gibran

PASSIONATE JOY IS CONNECTED TO love and friendship. What if we learned that the world was coming to an end? What if we had only five minutes left to say anything we wanted and needed to say? The cell phones would be ringing. All of us would want to contact somebody to say they something of love.

Why wait for the world to end before sharing words of love? Are we tongue-tied? We can unknot our tongues. We can tell our friends that we love them.

JOY HAS ITS REWARDS

The supreme reward of looking at life with a searchlight of happiness and the flashlight on a moment of joy comes at the end of each and every day. As we close our eyes to sleep, we can tell ourselves, "Joy has captured me today. I gave and received love and friendship." There is no better gift to ourselves and meaningful to others than to give part of ourselves. As we give out love, we make more friends and share our joy with many others, and it comes back to us in increasing measure.

That deep sense of satisfaction develops when we have given to another and received a response in return. This feeling inevitably rebounds, helping us more than others. Giving value to another is often joy enough. We have given with no concern for being misunderstood and without the need of reciprocity.

Those who give selfishly or reluctantly without caring for others will build instead of a wealth of joy, a prison around themselves. Giving in this spirit creates our own happiness as we treat those who will not give back to us with love. Giving is limited if we require a return. Building a wealth of joy requires finding our potential to give and receive, to build and maintain the joys.

LOVE RAISES CHEMISTRY

Anytime we have any degree of love, our brains secrete positive chemicals that enhance our happiness and natural living and coping abilities.

Love drives us to noble deeds. Love allows our spirit to push on against incredible odds. There is a huge difference inn loving what we do and liking what we do. Love creates passion. Love overcomes the option of quitting. Even when the times are tough, love prevails.

Love is the overflow of friendship. Not being loved results in misery. Those who have friends and those who love deeply never grow old. They die of old age, but they die young. We must have friends of every age, some older, some younger, especially the friendship of children.

To how many people in this love-starved world can we offer friendship and love? To everybody we meet. The capacity for friendship is limitless. Musicians speak of a life-long friendship between those who give out their art and those who listen.

When we extend or receive love and friendship, each of us is treating another as a respected equal. As we gaze toward another, we are looking into a mirror and seeing a reflection of ourselves. Whatever we give or withhold is reflected back to us. As we use our capacity for love and friendship, we enrich our own happiness each day.

Our ability to give and receive friendship and love makes us more alive. We are better able to attain happiness and joy. This discovery comes as we are open to love, willing to love. Risking friendship with another comes with an unwarranted fear of the consequences, not letting our stiff-necked pride get in the way, or our excess or false humility.

We keep ourselves aware and ready to give friendship and love with open minds, sound judgments, and an uncluttered spirit. We may use friendship as a drawing account, but we must never forget our own deposits.

TESTING OUR LOVE AND FRIENDSHIP

All of us try to give love and friendship generously. But how can we be certain? We could try a little exercise for a few weeks. Get out a notebook and list all of your acts of love and friendship. At the end of the day, as we prepare for a night's sleep, we can take a pen or pencil and actually write down what acts we have done. Check these over in your mind as you go to sleep.

Did we give somebody a kind word? Did we show appreciation for a task well done? Did we give helping hands? Did we go out of our way to be friendly? How did we lift another person's spirit? Did we keep a warm smile? Did we give compliments? Were we nice to the post office person, the grocer, the bank teller, and the gas station owner?

Keeping a notebook in which to list our acts of love, kindness, friendliness, appreciation, or consideration will enable us to evaluate each day. The list will grow longer each day, and we'll all be happier for the effort.

IT'S A WONDERFUL LIFE

This issue was addressed in the classic movie, *It's a Wonderful Life*. If you remember the film, Jimmy Stewart plays the main character, George Bailey. Although he was loved by most every person in the town of Bedford Falls, several circumstances kept George from leaving that town and fulfilling his dream of seeing the world.

One cold winter night when it looked like George's nemesis, Mr. Potter, was going to foreclose on George's bank debt, George became depressed and thought about jumping off a bridge to commit suicide.

In answer to a prayer he had offered earlier at a bar, God sent an angel named Clarence to show George what life in Bedford Falls would have been like if George had never been born.

George was reminded of the time his boss, Mr. Gower, a druggist, who was drunk and upset after learning that his son had been killed in the war, accidentally put poison in some medicine and told him to deliver the capsules to a family whose child was sick. Nothing bad happened because George realized what Mr. Gower had done and he never delivered that medicine.

However, in a replay of that event the sick child died because George was not there to stop the medicine from being delivered. Mr. Gower had to spend 20 years in prison and became a hopeless drunk because of what he had done.

George finally understood that everything good about his hometown was due in some way to his joyful, generous love and friendship to people in his town. Because he now understood, George was given the chance to live again so he could continue to be a friend.

CONNECTING WITH THOSE WE LOVE

Don't forget to nourish your relationships. No matter where we are, relationships take work. A faithful friend is the medicine of life. Use your new perspective for building a wealth of joy to strengthen the ties that are important to you.

Our valley times force us to slow down, examine our priorities, and make significant changes. We come face to face with the person we are moving quickly to get to know on deeper levels. First of all, that person is us. Low valley times shows us which friends really can be there for us and which ones, even if with good intentions, just cannot. We need to connect with positive people who will be our support as we ride the peaks and valleys.

The only way to make sure our networks do not break down in times of pain and suffering, disappointments and defeats is to tend to them, like a precious garden, every single day.

Life stressors threaten the most loving relationships. They leave us reeling when we need support. We feel like there's nothing to give. People don't view us as equals if they are our caretakers. Love means to keep talking, keep those lines of communication open as you accept the low times and anticipate more joy.

In the case of spouses, if the situation is left unchecked, the overtones of marriage can become drastically altered and the magic that brought us together will sail adrift.

All relationships change. If we continue to struggle to make our relationships what they were, we will never be able to see what they are, and what they will be.

LOVE DOES NOT FLY AWAY

Friendship has been called love without wings. It never flies away. Friendship is the cement of life that binds us together through mutual liking, sharing, and respect.

If we are extreme introverts with only one friend, no matter how far away, then we do not feel abandoned or lonely. If we are not connected to at least one human being who cares for us, then we experience pain that we are so aware of, it feels as strong as thirst or hunger. We starve with lack of friendship and love. Through this connection to friends, acquaintances—even strangers—we appreciate others and ourselves. Our own strengths build as we experience joy and personal worth.

To find a friend, we have to reach out, to offer friendliness. To be a friend is to gain a friend. If we have no friends, then we might not be giving much of ourselves. Perhaps we are not welcoming or receptive. Our world is filled with people starving for friendship and love. Millions are waiting for a friendly gesture from each of us. Share your joy times. Ralph Waldo Emerson once wrote, "Happiness is a perfume you cannot pour on others without getting a few drops on yourself." Catch those precious moments of joy while they are with us.

TO HAVE A FRIEND, BE A FRIEND

If we feel starved for friends, we must give friendship and we must keep on giving it. Friendship is understanding and communication between two or more people. Love and friendship grows when divided between two or more. Showing love and friendship will give back to us double, triple, and more, multiplying our own contributions. If we reach out to touch just one other person, we open a facet of life fully.

Friendship and love compound as we quit thinking and begin acting with a specific gesture. They do not exist in our minds alone. How many times have we said to another person, "Let's get together for lunch?" But unless we actually get in touch, that seed for a friendship will never grow.

Whose responsibility was that lost opportunity? It is our own, of course. We talked about it, but we did not follow through with action. Good intentions have no value unless fulfilled by effective deeds. The worst error we make in friendly connections is not to hate other people, but to be indifferent to them. Every day we meet people who are rude, crude, and indifferent toward us. That's the essence of inhumanity. Caring for others, reaching out, welcoming, helping, and accepting others will reveal the essence of humanity. By being a friend, we gain a friend.

Happiness comes as our efforts have proven to be of value to others. We become happy only through selfless giving and all of us are responsible for the rest of us. We get an exhilarating sensation when we share what we have. Moments of joy rush in. And another person is lifted from the bottom of life to the top. This is the truest essence of life, that deep gratification that comes when we touch another person with love and friendship. Of course, we can never correct all the wrongs, love all those who need it. But we can do our part. Just as the story of the man who was throwing struggling starfish back into the water, we don't look at the odds or how small our contributions are. Someone said, "What a waste. Millions of those starfish are going to die on the shore. You can't save them all." To that he said, as he threw another starfish into the ocean, "Well, it will make a difference to this one."

When we love and help others so that they are better for themselves, it's also better for us. A loving grandmother translated a grand thought as "do unto others as though you are the others." A memorable line in *My Fair Lady* says, "The difference between a lady and a flower girl is not how she behaves, but how she is treated."

As we add to the happiness of others, we add to our own. If at the end of your day, someone were to pay ten dollars for every kind, inspiring word you have spoken to others, and also collected ten dollars for all unkind, demeaning, hurtful words, would you be richer or poorer?

Love and friendship have no limits. The more we give and share, the more there is to use and absorb. For many of us life is going to a racetrack. We bet all our happiness on the pre-race favorite, which is called Hard Work. We feel betrayed when our horse fades down the homestretch and finishes out of the money. If we are to experience joy in the race of life, we need to place our bets on love and friendships, our relationships with others. Stephen Covey said that all of us have an emotional bank account. Words of praise, acts of kindness, enjoyable times spent together, our joys, are deposits we make into each other's accounts. Critical words, not keeping promises, deceit, lies, and not listening are withdrawals we make from those accounts. Think about any happy relationship that you have right now. In that one your deposits of love and friendship have far exceeded your withdrawals. Think about a relationship that is not going well or that has now ended. In that kind of relationship, the withdrawals were much more than your deposits.

FEELING JOY AS OUR SURPRISE IN THE SILENCE

Being willing to be vulnerable during times of surprise and silence is the spiritual key to permanent connection with ourselves. This act of acceptance will deepen and transform one to an abundant life. The more consciousness we direct into our soul, the higher its frequency becomes, much like light that grows brighter as we turn the dimmer switch and increase the flow of electricity. The more in touch one is by surrender by acceptance of all that life brings, the less negativity has power, and we tend to attract new circumstances that reflect life that is flowered with joy and happiness.

While we are waiting, we can use that time to commune with our Highest Power. Even traffic jams and lines become moments for inner joy. No matter what happens on the outside, nothing can shake us anymore. Being on top or bottom is irrelevant. My journeys to the bottom come quietly, as Sandburg wrote . . . "as little cat's feet." Rising to the bottom is not detectable by most of our friends or family. Like the buildings and uniforms and the fog in early morning at the United States Military Academy at West Point, our world may be covered with a blanket of gray. The sky could be royal blue. There could not be a cloud in the sky. We can use our time to shake off our mood like a dog shakes off rainwater, and move on.

Living without *passionate joy*, we become arrogant, stunted and dwarfed by easy relationships. And sadly we sing with that pop tune, "I don't know where we both went wrong, but the feeling's gone and I just can't get it back again."

It is a pleasure trip, an ecstatic high, a grand illusion, but the odds for that combination of circumstances to create anything real come at some other person's expense, and everything imagined as a wonderful life rescue ends up as self-defeating in the long run.

Trying to recapture such a joyous memory or happy time is impossibly unrepeatable. Those sets of circumstances can never again be reproduced. There's no joy in living in the present time on the basis of one of our memories that has now become a fantasy. Only then can we, like a tree that is rooted in the earth or a tall building with a deep and solid foundation, know happiness. Two men build houses. One man builds his house on sand, without a foundation. The storms and floods come, and his house is swept away. The other man digs and digs, struggles and struggles, until he reaches a solid rock. His house stands despite the floods and the power of the storms.

Close relationships are blighted, broken, and ended because our illusive concepts of "joy" as a human feeling become a command performance, a demand rather than a natural byproduct. Some of us become hostile, angry, bitter, and resentful because a brief period of emotional delight cannot be reproduced or ever perpetuated.

Our visions or concepts of joy have been hammered out in a thought out model, but practical pursuit of joy has been elusive. Joy comes as a person is free and faithful and quiet, free of coercion and demand. Joy comes as a product, not a production. It surprises the simplest person and eludes the sophisticated and the powerful. We have tried to buy joy. We have attempted to find it with body, soul, and spirit. Pursuing the pleasures of today, we cannot perceive tomorrow, but our tomorrow persistently arrives, and on that day, the demands for our paying the price for what we erroneously thought was joy, leave the lonely celebrant regretful, and bankrupt.

Building a wealth of joy in a world so starving causes us all to run in wrong directions, looking for love in all the wrong places. Moving or traveling to another place may promise to produce a joyous change and renewed hope. Our manic voyages take us to every part of the world. We spend too much money and time, all along thinking we are saving the world, but in reality perhaps we are competing with others to see more of the earth's diversity and building our résumés with more distinction. As Handel observed as he wrote his masterpiece, *The Messiah*, there is in sensual joys a hint of larger, nobler satisfaction, an emotional life experience that does endure. This joy endures to quench a deeper thirst. Despite his struggles with depression, Handel used his manic episodes to hear a voice of enhancing encouragement. He heard it in quiet moments of despair, during restless times of anxiety.

One of our long past clients had fallen to the bottom of her life. She came in desperation to do a series of sessions with us. Together each week we traveled on the difficult voyage through her bitterness, guilt, and fear. Her condition had caused many broken dreams. She was intelligent but dropped out of college to marry. It was then her dream-come-true. Then she experienced the nightmare of reality.

Jennifer (not her real name) discovered that her dream man was inconsiderate, mean, and selfish. His goal was ego-satisfaction. She and their children were pawns to his demands. His manly charm became brutishness. She tried to find a job. Her relationship to her controlling husband was hopeless to her. She enjoyed getting out of the house to work. She joined a sewing club. Building self-esteem, she was building her own life brick by brick. She dressed well. Mostly she wore a refreshing image like the one worn by some of her friends. She wept at her disappointments, her past pain.

Like all of us, she knew she was a straying sheep not worthy of happiness or times of joy. She did meet other Christian women whose lives were shallow as they used their "faith" as just another gimmick for self-gratification. She perceived herself as being at the center of the universe and that others were her servants. Her husband became angry. Both were confused and dismayed at the deepening break in their marital relationship. There were increasing tensions with their children. Eventually, with the help of therapeutic intervention, she made connections. Eventually, she left her job and returned to her home. She gave as much energy as she could to be a good wife and mother. She found joy in little things where she was and she never wanted to be anyplace else.

A man I'll call Jimmy Scott sought my wife out for counseling. Eventually, he brought his wife with him and we had a series of couple therapy sessions. Jimmy was head of a big department in a huge business firm. He told us that managers and those "rising to the top" play status-seeking games, sacrifice integrity for personal gains, and jostle each other for rank. Suspicion and fear colored the workplace. Hard workers with careful workmanship were devalued. His was just like the majority of business enterprises in the United States today.

Jimmy was diagnosed with schizoid affective disorder, but the company valued his work and gave him accommodation to go for therapy, retreat from the daily grind, and gain perspective. He wanted to be a justice maker, a problem solver. He communicated in no uncertain, sometimes angry and profane terms, as he elbowed his way into a hearing and voiced his protests. He was courageous indeed, but he came to see that his efforts were tinged by self-righteousness. If others under him were wrong, and they were, then he thought it was his duty to judge. This elevation of his true self after many years built feelings of superiority. Jimmy found that people refuse to be corrected from a pedestal. His wife agreed and gave the insight that that was the basis of their many problems with their children. Jimmy finally was able to accept his situation. He now knew that he could not take responsibility for that whole business firm or even his department, despite his lot in life.

He's still angry, but he is starting to realize that his angry protests, argumentative strivings, and mean-spirited derision are not the pathway to restoring integrity to his workplace or his home life. If he did not change, the stress would undo him, and he would lose not only his credibility but also his integrity and leadership.

DON'T POSTPONE JOY OR LET IT PASS YOU BY

Did you hear that car passing by your home or office? Did you hear the dog bark? Do you hear somebody in the house? Can you hear the gift of peace in those sounds? Well, I can't either. Look for peace in the silence out of which the sounds come and into which they return. Pay close attention to the silence than to the sounds. Paying attention to the outer silence creates inner silence. Our minds become quiet. Peace can come to us all.

Sounds come out of silence. Every sound dies back into silence, which is surrounded by silence. Silence enables sound to be. Life is present in our world as silence. Pay attention. Nothing is closer to happiness than silence. Listen to the sounds of silence between words. Let stillness surround us. Nobody can be still within without giving attention to the gift of silence.

In a moment of surprise, a drop of water falls on one's joy-ful center. Another drop falls. Feelings arrange themselves in order around us, and then we finally feel the warmth. Memories and thoughts line up like soldiers in proper order. Joy feelings mingle with the guilt, the anxiety, the anger, and the fear. It's all part of our living. In time our painful memories of the never-ending darkness transform into compassion for others, as the victim is both wiser and deeper than at any time of living.

We share a constant reminder that another self-defeating episode could be cast upon us. The only choice is to live a full life every day. We cannot create joy, but we can be prepared for its gift, not when we may have wanted it but when we needed it most. Life is not a problem we can solve, but a mystery we can enjoy.

All of us need a private place. Here, we find where we can create an atmosphere for revivifying serenity and silence. Here, we remember our times of joy. John Maxwell tells us that he has a "thinking chair" in a quiet room of his own home. For you, your private place may be under a tree on soft green grass, or on a park bench. We all need a private place.

In our private places we can escape the distractions from people who are rude, crude, and indifferent. Here we can go on a voyage of discovery. Instead of regretting our loneliness, we can make the most of it. Silence here gives peace of mind. The healing quiet will refresh our minds and will strengthen that inner spirit that will reward us as we are surprised by joy. We will have no regrets for slowing down in our private place. We owe ourselves the soul-mending quiet time at least once each day. Schedule it into your life whenever possible in early morning, at twilight, just before sleep, whenever it fits best.

MAINTAINING LOVE AND FRIENDSHIPS

When friends are out of touch for long periods of time, they just can't wait to talk to each other. This often is the case when we need to reflect on where life is going for us.

Most of the directives and advice we receive daily are conflicting and distressful. Nothing can relieve the tension that we feel as much as an open conversation with a friend who understands us.

We don't want to risk sharing ourselves with a stranger. An unknown person might manipulate or seduce us. A loving friend creates for both of us a relaxing atmosphere in which we can talk in confidence about doing or not doing a task, going or not going where we think the joy is.

FRIENDSHIP REQUIRES DEDICATED EFFORT

Maintaining love and friendships takes a lifetime of dedicated effort. The gift of befriending challenges friends to face with honesty what might cause stress even between themselves. Friends pledge to each other that they will deal with life's hills and valleys. Friends explore creatively how theory can treat each other with gentleness as well as firmness when necessary. The love they feel for one another helps them preserve the integrity of their relationship.

At times our friends may feel worked up by a minor crisis, by an upset in the family, in the workplace, or somewhere in their personal world. Deep appreciation causes us to co-experience what our friends are thinking and feeling. To appreciate a friend's experience with genuine empathy is not a matter of nodding politely or explaining any problem and its solution intellectually. We are affected by whatever is happening to the one for whom we care. And our friends will feel understood by us.

When others are rude, crude, and indifferent; when they wound us; or when we wound them, we need a friend to help us sort out what has happened. Friends are like two thirsty people crossing a desert looking for a refreshing oasis.

An encouraging word goes a long way. A friend will find, as if by magic, the right word we need to hear. The word to us may be verbal or non-verbal. The message may come from a touch of a hand, an encouraging smile, a bear hug.

Friends are a source of joy in each other's life. Sharing joys makes the times doubly meaningful. Though friends endure painful times of growth, they never deliberately cause each other pain. Friends are the apple in each other's eye. They rejoice in each other by sharing a meal, taking a walk, or offering to do mutual favors.

Friendship happens not because of a sense of duty or obligation, but for the enjoyment of being together. Friendship is a source of lasting joy. That is why the loss of a friend through an accident or death, is a loss from which we never fully recover. Mourning does not wipe out the missing.

We can think about the miner who saved his friends by slowing down time in the minds of his friends. The passing of each minute was precious to them. He bore the pain of bearing the struggle of the extra, unspoken hours by himself.

If we do not experience this joy when we are together, the friendship itself may die or slowly become unstitched. It may then become a once upon a time friendship.

To maintain the friendship, we express to each other whenever we are able the joy we feel about a shared success or a difficulty overcome. The richest person in the world is not the one who still has the first dollar that they ever earned. It's that joyous person who still has their first friend.

PRACTICING CHRISTIAN FRIENDSHIP

In the first chapter of Mark's gospel (1:40–45) we read that Jesus uses spiritual power to heal a man with leprosy. If we impose our understanding of medicine in our century and call Jesus the great physician who removes a source of suffering, we miss the point. So we think that Jesus functioned as a surgeon does today, but without antibiotics or equipment.

We realize that Jesus was a friend to those who needed compassion. We focus on the disease that kept the man from enjoying life. We must also look at the meaning of leprosy. In Jesus's time, a person living with leprosy was "unclean." He suffered from being excluded from friendship. He could not even attend the synagogue. When Jesus touches him, he becomes polluted with the social and spiritual stigma. Jesus shifts the boundaries. His friendship with this man caused "the least of these" to form the heart of the kingdom of God.

Those religious people who marginalized the "unclean" find that they themselves are the marginalized and cut off from God. They now view Jesus as part of a "social death." Jesus is alienated from the religious environment that eventually was shown in his crucifixion. And so our choice of whom to show friendship toward is an indication of our faith.

To have a disease such as bipolarity or schizophrenia in our day is also to be stigmatized, alienated, friendless, and prevented from expressing faith. Mental illness is a total, whole person plague. The mentally ill become "bipolars" or "schizophrenics" or even "crazies," "hopelessly insane," or the "loonies." All their experiences with life are interpreted through a lens of our assumptions about the mentally ill. Because these sufferings tend to be negative, so the social identification of the person is negative.

Even in the call of God to serve, the person's spiritual experiences are interpreted by ideas of pathology. Mental health centers exclude spirituality expression as pathological and they actively seek to disengage any form of spirituality from therapy. Most denominations will include policies and procedures that eliminate those with mental illness from being ordained into ministry. We realize this pattern of exclusion from their community, personal relationships, and God just like the experience of people with leprosy during the time of Jesus.

The friendships that Jesus created with people revealed that they deserved friendship with God. This is our model as to how the practice of friendship can ease the suffering of the mentally ill living in our neighborhoods and desiring to find a spiritual home.

Friendships are critical for physical, psychological, and spiritual health. From friends we receive a meaning and purpose for living, a sense of identity, and ultimate significance. Friendships express love, bring happiness, and moments of joy.

People in our day don't want to share their wealth of anything, much less the building of a world with an environment for love and joy. Being friends in our day means social exchange or even likeness. Friends are people that we can gain things from, such as position, money, or pleasure. If the friendship is personally satisfying, we keep at it; but if not, we drop them flat. If one friendship is lacking, we find another. We assume that a friend must be like us. We have to share common interests, political interests, and social activities. Jesus had friends out of his love and grace. He was friends with people who were radically different, such as sinners, the unclean, women, and tax collectors. They were persons to him, unbounded by assumptions.

All of us have some mental, physical, or spiritual disabilities. Whatever is wrong with any of us, a whole lot is wrong with all of us just a little bit. We say, "We just don't have the ability to cope with ill people." Yet to cut off the possibility of community care with negative expressions is to hide behind stigmatizing labels and prejudices that prevent us from friendships with those who suffer. Mental health problems first are human experiences before they become diagnoses. In making friends with people living with serious illnesses, there will be moments of frustration, joy, sadness, and uncertainly. But if we do not offer such friendships, who will?

PRACTICAL APPLICATION

1. Attend a Recovery, Inc. meeting or any self-help group composed of people with a passion for overcoming any problem.

2. What to do when joy appears impossible:

+ Accept all your feelings as part of who you are. Avoid using pleasure or counterfeit joy or checking out to escape pain.

+ Own your negative and painful feelings. Embrace them. Do not permit them to control you.

+ Resolve conflict with others. Refuse to create an environment with your friends and others that yields an undercurrent of anger or hostility.

+ Identify any other joy killers. Decide how you will eliminate them.

+ Share with at least two people your passions for living.

XI

JOY AND THE VOCATION
OF BEAUTY

There is no beautifier of complexion, or form, or behavior, like the wish to scatter joy and not pain around us.

— Ralph Waldo Emerson

SOME OF US PRACTICE A vocation of beauty. This is neither a job for you, nor does it mean you have to make music or become an artist. Beauty seen and appreciated is never lost. Beauty cannot exist for us if we permit our eyes and minds pass over the opportunities in an unseeing way. Do not let joy pass you by. Beauty, like joy, that is not perceived is lost forever.

Beauty is seen with awe and gratitude in church architecture, great government buildings, castles, and stadiums. We can view a rock in the forest or even colors of glass in jars, bottles, and chips of broken glass. Our children pick cloverleaves, daisies, or wild flowers to beautify our homes. At Christmas, a little boy ran to look under the tree. There, he saw his old dark blue Noxzema jar. He played with it for several minutes before realizing there were other beautiful things under the tree.

One woman said she was feeling depressed one day but was stopped in her tracks by a scarlet maple tree. The beauty of the leaves cleansed her spirit. Some say beauty is the holiness of

God. The *Oxford Dictionary* defines beauty as a combination of color, shape, and so on that pleases the senses. Also, beauty is an excellent specimen, elegance, loveliness, attractiveness, or aestheticism.

Beauty is difficult to define. We know that beauty is that which connects our innermost being to the outer world, giving us an experience of joy and peace simultaneously. Beauty is exhilarating. Beauty increases our sense of being alive; but beauty is so serene, imparting the sense of timelessness, which is why we speak of beauty as being eternal.

Perception of the beauty around us is important in realizing joy. Art is one area we can explore. We don't have to be able to draw or paint anything of beauty, but we can experience it, really see it. We need an open intelligence and a will to make the effort.

We can read some fine art books. We can see for ourselves paintings and sculptures through reproductions. We can go to a museum. Another world is there waiting for us.

Beauty and moments of joy are available through music, the speech of angels.

There is beauty in many types of music including opera, orchestral, instrumental, classical, popular, country. Music is eternal. Horace called music a "sweet healing balm of troubles" in 50 BC. Music created centuries ago can bring us enjoyment today.

The beauty of music is not found only in the concert hall or even in our homes. We can enjoy music in the outdoors, in the whirring wings and song of a passing bird, the sigh of a spring breeze through the petals of a flower. Soothing music flows through the tinkling fall of rain. Beauty in all forms of art passes feelings from one person to others. Art does not reproduce just what we see. The beauty of art is that it makes us see.

FINDING JOY IN NATURE

Another place for the beauty of art, music, and poetry is in all growing things. Anyone who has wisdom will spend time in contemplating nature's beauty. What innocent joy in finding a four-leaf clover, an undiscovered waterfall, a unique rock, or a special flower. Next time you walk out into nature, look at a flower. Study the details of the petals, pistils, and leaves. We will experience a tranquil joy. Like Saint Francis of Assisi, we can speak to nature. Talk, sing, and croon to the plants and the water. Put your feet in a creek or stream.

When life gets us down, even for a day or two, we can always turn our eyes upward and outward, take a deep breath, and enter the stillness of nature. We can just stand in wonder before nature's natural beauty. From the tiniest gnat to the tallest mountain peak, nature helps us live the mystery.

The beauty our eyes see in a natural winter landscape frees us from loud stress to the peacefulness of relaxing to surprising times of joy. Nature never loses its radiance.

We can find it in a sunrise. No two are the same. Each of us can discover a different color. Watch a bird in flight, especially a powerful hawk or an eagle. Observe a powerful storm, rampaging with strength. Listen with awe to the song of the sea as waves lick the shore in perfect rhythm. Nature puts life in proper perspective making room for joy. Nature is part of the joyful dance of life.

It is not only a feast for the eyes that nature gives. If we open our emotional response to nature's lessons, we will acquire a wisdom only hinted at in the words of philosophers. We experience the endurance of a bare tree shivering through icy blasts into spring lushness. We take in the rush-flow of a stream suddenly dammed up by boulders, yet patiently and beautifully eddying around obstacles. We come upon the softness of a past-its-prime flower petal withering with a sad yet sweet gesture. Joy in nature is infinite. Nature's joy connection reminds us that we dwell in times and seasons of life-giving joy from youth to maturity, from planting time to harvest, in the company of others or by ourselves.

Paying attention to nature yields sweet rewards such as the sight of plants sprouting and trees budding, the sounds of birds singing and insects buzzing, the touch of wind on our faces, and the disappearing act of the snow. The fragrant flowers, the singing birds, the blossoming trees give us an invitation to find joy and healing in the beauty of our natural world.

SAVING THE WEALTH OF THE EARTH

We inflict so much pain on our living place. With every tree we cut down, with the poison we put into earth's atmosphere, with every death of an animal at the hand of a human, and the callous leveling of land and place once natural to make way for development, the earth is hurt again and again. Rainforests are destroyed each year, equaling an area 30 times larger than the state of Connecticut. Our oceans are polluted and overfished, and the beautiful coral reefs are dying. Annually, the ozone layer is weakened. Global warming will eventually bring rising seas and climatic change. Building a wealth of joy in our world means we must change. If not we will bring about the most destruction ever experienced by humankind. We are the last generation to have the possibility of pulling ourselves out of the mess we made.

Human beings and other animals were placed within nature. Throughout all our years of existence on this beautiful planet, we have lived in nature. We are a part of nature. Without our joy instinct we will become unnatural. Our survival depends on nature. Nature was not designed to be plundered by us. The more we take from the earth, the more impoverished we will be. Without a wealth of joy, we have become love starved, isolated, and alone. We have taken on more loneliness. We have gotten more isolated, alone, surrounded and chocked by crowds of other humans. Disconnected from the whole, we have acted as if we were above all other life. The reality is that we have become tragically and painfully separate from divine nature.

Sacred beauty has been defiled. Some distorted spirituality has exposed a doctrine of separation, making it orthodox to claim the earth and its animals as belonging to them. That distorted error has caused a narrow and hypocritical religious observance. The cult springing ever from distortion of the major religions of earth has led us to become selfish and unfulfilled. Materialism will never bring happiness.

Nothing was created to be separate from the whole. Walking in the cool of the garden of earth equals loneliness of spirit and with loneliness of spirit comes disconnection. Because we do not connect, sometimes we die within. Daily, humans walk an unnatural path to nowhere. Without a life purpose to being joy to the world, we are lost to the whole, and we find that we have become spiritually, mentally, and physically isolated from the natural whole. Loving the earth is about transition to a higher spiritual plane.

We have bought into the myth of human supremacy by misunderstanding our faith and even our religious literature. Muslim, Christian, Jewish, and other mean-spirited ultra fundamentalists recommend wholesale destruction by destroying the beauty of the earth and even each fellow human as their way of life.

Can we deny that in Christian America, we persecuted and impoverished Native Americans and animals and their homes? The loss and pain we delivered to nature was unimaginable. There was a kinship of all life and a similarity of belief about the sacredness of the earth. Each tribe was of the same race, but with distinctive and differing understandings about spirituality. But no tribe had as their purpose the destruction of the land. During a speech near Standing Bear Lake in Omaha, Nebraska, a Lakota descendent of Standing Bear, said, "Forests were mowed down, the buffalo exterminated, the beaver driven to extinction. The white man is the symbol of extinction for all things natural." Killing the beasts was the same as killing spirit. We are like strangers taking what is not ours to take. Earth was not something to be bought and sold. If we do not change, our appetite will destroy the earth.

Our distorted religious beliefs do not allow us to be part of nature, but rather we are apart from it. We see nature as something from which to extract what humankind perceives as wealth to be used for our own selfish reasons. The knowledge and respect of the connection of humans and nature has been distorted and then lost, perhaps forever.

HEALING OUR WOUNDED SELVES

We need to look inside where our joys are stored if healing is to happen. We need to shed tears of grief and repentance for the violence done to nature. We need to cry for the alienation and losses we have experienced in our lives today, not just in generations of our ancestors past. Only then can sorrow be replaced by a wealth of joy. What a *jouissance* that would be. This would be a loving joy, a joy of feeling free and guiltless. Again we could identify ourselves, our very souls, with the beauty of nature. We can again connect with an honest theology of earth. Our action can become the antithesis to environmental values, or our lack of values, which have existed for too long. Building a wealth of joy in a world starved for love can become a turning point. The path for reconnection lies in front of us.

We are never completely lost so long as we claim kinship with everything that is. We can feel this joy as we view the sun on colored fall leaves, a beautiful sunset, or the beauty of snowflakes falling from the sky.

We cannot only heal ourselves, but we can be part of healing the wounds of others. We must find ways to reconnect with the earth and all its beautiful creation. Connection is possible. It is not that far away from us. Some of us have started. We tend to our plants and gardens. We care for pets for companions. We drive for miles to enjoy natural surroundings. Nature can soothe the troubled heart. Plants and animals can refresh our souls. Nature will calm the weary, soften the hardened, and redirect the lost. We will begin to see God in everything. We will view all things in nature as members of one whole community.

To build a wealth of joy is really up to us. Most people deep down have a joy instinct that neither harms others nor destroys the earth. No matter what your faith understanding is, we know it is wrong to destroy, to create suffering, to take what belongs to another, to kill or to be the cause of something or someone that is killed. Even if we never stepped inside a church or mosque or synagogue, we know a smile is better than a grimace. We know that caring is good and selfishness is not. Within any human awareness, it feels right to be kind and wrong to feel malice or anger. We just have to listen to our inner voice, the joy instinct.

Building a wealth of joy means to live with ethical considerations globally before acting. The rainforests would not be felled. Our seas would not be polluted. We would not inflict our earth with wars or calamities that we have created with our own agendas.

If we would go with our joy instinct, we would enjoy a calmer, quieter, and ecologically healed world around us. Some are responding to their inner voice. Some speak out in a whisper, others with a clarion call. We can heal the earth.

EMBRACING THE BEAUTY OF LIFE

We know beauty when we encounter it. Our knowledge of beauty may be objective. Our comprehension of beauty is not objective. When we say with surprising passion, "That's beautiful," what we are saying is, "That causes a startling joy response in us." Beauty is old and young all at once. Beauty will dance with any of us who are brave enough to ask her.

Once we find joy and beauty within, our world becomes infused with it. More than any other emotion, beauty is close to our joy response.

In the midst of an experience of beauty, we instinctively become silent. It's like a hush comes over us when we walk into a great cathedral. Some part of us will recognize that we are in the presence of something holy. Poet e. e. cummings describes that beauty in saying, "Now the eyes of my eyes are opened." Beauty captures our attention, lifting us out of ourselves, and surprising us with joy.

When we drive someplace like the Sandhills of western Nebraska, we realize slowly how peace is penetrating into our bones. Whatever happens next in our lives, even if our worst fears should put us in a valley of despair, life goes on. As long as nature continues, as long as there are sand hill cranes and miles of enchanting lands and beauty, life will continue forever for us all. Beauty in any unique natural area yields harmony when life fits together, as in the design of the human body.

When we look up the word beauty in books or on the Internet, we find mostly articles about bodies, especially bodies of women. Beauty is to be embraced. As we reflect on our bodies something surprising happens. We can feel appreciation for all the places of our bodies, for the memories it stores, and for the secrets it keeps. Evidences of broken bones may remind us of the joy of playing at sports. We can recall the pleasure our bodies have given to us and for passion expressed as our lovers find moments of joy within the hills and valleys. We are all blessed with such beautiful temples.

Elisabeth Kübler-Ross wrote, "People are like stained glass windows. They sparkle when the sun is out, but when the darkness sets in, their true beauty is revealed only if there is a light from within."

We can make peace with our current reflection as we look at photographs of the many extraordinary faces that have evolved during our lifetimes. Embrace those lines that stare back at us, those parts that sag in the middle or stick out. We have no need to copy or clone others that we have admired. We just wanted to fit in. We were made to stand out.

BEAUTY LEAPS BARRIERS

Beauty has the power to leap barriers that we build to separate ourselves from each other. We could be on the bow of a cruise ship watching a brilliant sunset. We would be awed as the hot tangerine sun sinks into the ocean. And next to you might be a man from Iraq; next to that person was someone from the Netherlands; and next to that one was a person from France. We would be sharing a common experience of beauty. Beauty transcends human differences.

For the first time in history, human beings are able to see the earth as a totality, transcending the barriers of nations. The photographs taken by astronauts in space give us this image of our planet as a whirling ball with shimmering gold on the side next to the sun, shading into blues and greens, turning slowly in the inky blackness of space.

When the crew of Apollo 8 looked out of their spaceship and saw all of their home earth for the first time, one of them said, "My God, it's so beautiful."

PRACTICAL APPLICATION

Name what you consider as beauty.

Stop worrying about things you cannot control. List them.

1.

2.

3.

4.

5.

6.

7.

Do something about something you can change . . . you. List what you can do.

1.

2.

3.

4.

5.

6.

7.

Describe how you will be flexible, trusting things beyond your control to those who make those choices.

XII

GIVE YOURSELF A BREAK

He who binds to himself a joy
Does the wingéd life destroy;
But he who kisses the joy as it flies
Lives in eternity's sunrise.

— William Blake

A S YOU READ, PERHAPS YOU may still feel like you are escaping the dark doldrums. Don't let the present moment pass you by. Experience the full force of experiencing your now. Take a walk. Breathe deeply. Gaze at the trees and the beauty of nature. Listen to the birds. Look up into the sky. Take in the beauty around you. Go eat your favorite food. Savor each bite as you transition from where you are now. Peel an orange or grate a lemon and smell the rind. Hug your child. Thank a friend. Ask forgiveness from those you hurt. Look into a mirror and accept yourself. See your hope as you smile. Did you notice? Go to a quiet place. Express your emotions. Give thanks for your soul made for endurance.

Before you read further, brace yourself for the struggles that are yet to come. How do you feel right now? Are you tired? Are you overwhelmed? Close this book and close your eyes. Take a few minutes in your most comfortable chair or your thinking place, or rest your head on a desk or table. Go to bed early tonight. And take a nap Sunday afternoon. Don't worry.

Your joy will come to you. So will the rest of your life.

PRACTICAL APPLICATION

Read again the first chapters.

Buy a copy for a friend.

XIII

OUR STRUGGLE NEVER ENDS

There is no pain so great as the memory of joy in present grief.

—Aeschylus

J OY INCLUDES SUFFERING. OUR LIFE struggles are never-ending. Battles for happiness must constantly be waged. One of our common mistakes when we seek to come back from a tragic valley experience is to assume that our struggle has an end. It doesn't. Our valley times can last a year or longer. But sooner or later the intensity of our suffering will subside.

However, the subsequent struggle for healing and restoration in our lives is endless. The world is the closed door. It is the love-starved reality. When joy is experienced and as we become happy in the midst of suffering, the world becomes a passageway to joy everywhere. The relationship between joy and suffering is a part of what we call the problem of evil. We observe that any attempt in human experience to be happy, to known times of joy will involve suffering. Joy and suffering are by no means mutually exclusive.

Of course, there is the pathology known as masochism, in which intense pleasure is derived from intense pain, so that pain is sought for the pleasure it brings. But there is no masochism in the suffering that is uninvited. We cannot stop our suffering completely even when it's over. Our capacity for suffering is the inevitable concomitant of the capacity for joy. Suffering is the twin sister of joy.

We dance with the pain and suffering times. An incurable invalid who has fully accepted the suffering of his constriction may do more to establish justice in the world than a host of bustling reformers. The invalid can empower others to do joyous work.

Sometimes we make it through the first stage of suffering. We breathe a sign of relief. We say to ourselves, "At last it's over. I can get on with my life now." Then we look in front of us and we realize that we are not equipped to enter the life that lies before us.

It is easy to lose all hope, especially when we have worked so hard to reach a certain point or goal, only to confront another roadblock. When we feel trapped, we think there is no way out of our predicament. But there is indeed a transition through any obstacle. We have to find the courage to "go for it." We press on even when it appears we have made no progress.

If we are ever to build *jouissance*, we have to have the will to effort, to push on into our unknown future. There will be new challenges to face and some will set us back. But if we stop trying and give in to despair, we stop living. We need the skills to stare down adversity and to gain the faith to face whatever may come without fear and without despair.

OUR ASSUMPTIONS THAT LIFE GETS BETTER AND BETTER

We might be tempted to think that we'll not hit the bumps in life's road. Our world has told us that the economy, our careers, and our culture would get better year by year, generation by generation. Our families have told us that if we follow the cultural rules, we would transition to better and better lives.

Work hard. Get a college diploma. Eventually, we'll arrive at a steady and upward climb to security. This might have made sense when life did not contain so much turmoil, dishonesty, and change. Life is a self-renewing process with many ups and downs. Our lives are measured by cycles and chapters, not by accomplishments in a permanent upward trend. Our lives are stories with hills and valleys.

We must remain oriented to the future, drawing upon our emergent vision and energy. Times of depression are not the opposites from times of joy. Perhaps energy and vision are lacking during times of pain and depression. We have to embrace our transitions when they happen, and use them for renewal and discovery.

How we handle life's endings determines our happiness. Disenchanted things happen to us. It is then that we are out of sync. Of course, we become angry. We express pessimism, restlessness, denial, and we worry about where others are and what they think about us.

Simon and Garfunkel sang, "Slow down, you move too fast." The worst sufferings in life cause us to tap our core values, to explore. We slow down to heal, to find a quiet place to do some inner work. Everyone needs a time to be a human being and not just a human doing. Treasure the times you can get off the racetrack. If you are in a valley time, get ready, a hill time, a time of joy will soon come into our lives.

Passion is a word that we can use as we get ready for going "where the joy is." We get ready by sensing a new purpose. We learn to network with others. We can set ourselves on fire to use our creativity. Then as in the action movies, we go for it. We are energized, optimistic, active, and committed heroes. We become as Willie Nelson sang, "on the road again."

Each new day brings a new struggle. The most persistent struggles are the least dramatic ones. Struggles during a life-threatening illness are not as difficult as something that drags our spirits down. It is really not the loss of our jobs, but it is the daily pressures of work. It is not the struggle during a divorce, but the constant struggle to sustain and revitalize a marriage. It is not the struggle at the death of a loved one, but the hostile relationship we struggle to repair. We must continue on a healing path when our lives are constantly in turmoil.

OUR LIVES SPIN OUT OF CONTROL

Sometimes life spins out of control. All our efforts to move on toward a higher plane fail. The whole world seems to be conspiring against us. We think we are jinxed.

Our personal truth is that we are losing perspective. Sure we are overworked, losing sleep, eating harmfully. Life's blessings are all around us but we don't slow down to see them. Each day life offers another challenge. There will be inevitable setbacks. We might lose our footing and fall back down again. We have to force ourselves to understand how far we have come and what wonderful things we have learned. We have the power and the skills to make each transition. This valley time will pass. And we will find ourselves climbing higher and higher toward our dreams and plans and life purpose.

Down in our valleys, our valleys so low, we don't always discover just one painful event or happening. Suffering is often the result of a long accumulation of frustration and unhappiness. Disaster came but nothing really changed. We can't hang on to a single misfortune. We can't really find a hook on which to hang our sorrow. We can't communicate the source of our pain. Every day we find ourselves with enigma of anger, bitterness, and tired. We are in the valley again, but we can't find the cause of it.

Maybe we are in a grieving time for all the potential that we failed to realize. Perhaps all the compromises we have been forced to make during our lifetime have caught up with us. Perhaps suddenly we think our lives have no meaning. We feel we are in a state of shallow, passionless existence. Or just maybe we have become painfully aware of how little time we have left and how much we continue to hope to accomplish.

An unlived life is a tragedy. But we have in us a power to remake ourselves, to climb out of the valley toward the joy we perceive that is just on top of the hill. Could we actually uncover our passion? Could we overcome our fears? Could we still realize our dreams?

When we think about potential, we think of children. We see a child and we say that this one's going to be a lawyer, or that little boy will be a musician. But rarely do we speak about potential when we are thinking about ourselves. Some days we sense that there is still a would-be-if-I-could-be, could-be-if-I-would-be syndrome in each of us, but this thinking gets more anxiety-provoking the more we contemplate what we have to lose.

We see ourselves as fully formed. So we dismiss our hopes

and dreams as mere fantasies. We assume that the time for realizing all that we can be is passed. But no matter what our age, we have the potential to grow and to change.

To transform ourselves we have to look honestly at ourselves and experience our dissatisfaction. We have to allow ourselves to fully feel our hunger for a joyous life. Another prerequisite for transforming ourselves is the ability to excavate a deeply held longing. If we are unhappy and starved for love, we have no place to go. Change means risk-taking. We must be willing to leave the security of our lives behind and journey to an uncertain future. We have to be willing to face another failure as we step into the unknown.

TRANSFORMING EMOTIONS

Positive emotions elevate our chemistry. Our struggles are easier. Our natural abilities increase. The more skilled we become at transforming our negative emotions into joy, the more purpose driven and happier we'll become.

Everything we experience in life is a mere triviality. Life experiences are historical facts. It is the negative emotions we attach to our facts that keep us from becoming happy people with life purposes.

Getting up at five o'clock in the morning to exercise is a fact. If we just hate getting up early, we have no motivation to get out of bed when the alarm rings. Getting our sleep is also a fact. Only if we decide to move our muscles will we gain the personal satisfaction of getting up to exercise instead of focusing on our disposition to stay in bed. We can focus on getting into shape, looking better, and being in charge of our life videos.

How can we do it? We have to transform our emotional

association to the life facts. We do it by changing our focus. It is much easier if we pay close attention to the joy instinct, to positive thoughts instead of negative, endorphin-depriving thinking.

A bull rider gets a special euphoric feeling by being one with a two-ton out-of-control animal. Most of us would have a time connecting to the joy of riding that bull, enjoying the flow of eight eternal seconds being in complete control. Bull riders tell us that succeeding in that ride is their biggest rush in life.

Creating positive emotions, love, and courage allow us to push on in spite of our discomfort. This creation causes our brain to release chemicals that block out pain and give us additional energy. Not many of us would ride a bull. Some have experienced the "runner's high" by pushing themselves beyond pain and fatigue until their brains release endorphins, a chemical with properties much similar to those in morphine.

As we find ourselves in situations that approach our pain threshold, we can realize that pain is a "fact." We can choose how we wish to experience them emotionally. We can choose to focus all our attention on the pleasure we receive from controlling our life videos. We are in control of our life destiny. Happiness is our reward for pushing ourselves beyond what other people are willing to do.

Remember, every video in your mind is a "fact." While we cannot control facts, we can control our response to them. As we do, we will have more fun and experience more joys.

What it takes is a conscious effort to realize that an emotionally negative response to a fact of our living, fair or unfair, poisons our chemistry and hinders us. If we can completely understands that negative emotional responses contribute to our unhappiness and failures, we can transform those negative videotapes into positive ones by simply changing our focus. We must work at it, over and over again. There will be setbacks, but soon, it becomes an instinctive habit.

Mistakes are experiences to learn from. We can make adjustments to them and do better next time. Another Confucius quotation: "He who conquers himself is the mightiest warrior."

We must pay a price if we are to experience a transformation. Some of us will have to listen to and then ignore the many people who will tell us what a dreadful mistake we are making. It is hard enough to step beyond self-doubt when taking a risk with the future. And when those closest to us start criticizing us, we have to gather up enormous courage not to be swayed by their assessments of us.

We might even face shame or gossip or ostracism from our family or peers. The cost of realizing our dreams and building a wealth of joy is high, but the rewards are immeasurable.

Some of us experience unhappiness and frustration not because of our own failure, but because others prohibited them from realizing our callings. One woman was gifted with talents for music, but her dad never allowed her to pursue her gift. He wanted her to find a profitable moneymaking career path. Hundreds of people whose deep longings have been thwarted by their family, by a discriminatory society, or even by faith groups stay in their valleys.

It is never too late to recapture our passionate longings and to realize their realities. By breaking down the barriers that others have placed in our path, we cannot only set out for a new future, but we can also rectify wrongs committed against us in our past.

Every one of us is specially blessed with many talents, and it is our task to realize them. Never underestimate your potential. Never lose hope. Find the strength to keep on trying, the courage to be different, and embrace the energy to give all that we have been given to offer to the world. Unexpected miracles are standing right in front of us. Why can't we see them? We ignore the possibilities for joy with closed eyes. We must uncover what we have forsaken to find what we have been searching for. We do not have to travel far away to discover something beautiful and new for miracles surround us.

Keep on growing with your new insights. There are steps we can take that might heighten our awareness of joy, when all we see is life's daily struggles. When we go through the dark valley times we wonder if we are ever going to experience another joy.

During a normal time of no hills or valleys, we lean on daily distractions to lesson the sting of our struggle. The world around us becomes still. Our world around us begins to stir. Our inner world is filled with turmoil. We would prefer not to deal with the thoughts that come to us. We attempt to ignore our feelings. Perhaps we perceive that we must have two personalities. During our joy times, we are confident, rational, and so grateful. But in the valley times, we become vulnerable and shaky.

DREADED VALLEYS LEAD TO JOY

As much as we dread the valleys, they can teach us the steps to joy.

Struggling through the valley experiences teaches us humility. They remind us that we are vulnerable, that we are small and frail and mortal. We are just a part of nature's unchanging rhythm. We would like to defy its pull, but we must eventually give in to the struggle and pain that eventually comes to all of us.

No matter how many lights we have on or how long we stay up and watch late night television or how much we run into pleasure's arm, we have to inevitably concede and continue the struggle.

Low times in life show us that we are more complicated than we think. We can create new visions and dreams or we can give in to our capacity to wish for terrible things. Valley times create an atmosphere for prayer times. During our successful high times, most of us rarely feel the need or the time to pray. During the valleys, all of us whisper secrets to God as if to a close friend. We are then more sensitive to the spirit, to miracles.

During valley times we are forced to regroup, to reflect, and to rest. This step might be called our cocooning time. Dark valleys remind us of the womb from which we all emerged. Valley times urge us to remember that we can recreate ourselves out of that womb-like darkness. During this step to joy we face our deepest fears. We do what we fear the most to do.

There is a problem during this valley step. We might be reborn in the valley, but when the morning comes out from our mourning, we pretend nothing has happened to us. We wipe the tears from our eyes. We dismiss the fears out of the recesses of our minds and all those prayers from the depths of our souls. Only when we embrace the side of us that dwells in darkness and pain can we experience life with an openness to perceive and to receive the blessings that are within reach every day. There is nothing in the valley that we cannot face. Nothing will be given to us that we do not have the capacity to bear. Valley times magnify our struggles, but we know that we can have better days. Trust that the struggles will give way to more *passionate joy*.

We live in the valley times at our own pace. We accept the plight and keep our expectations realistic. If we move in easy, slow, manageable steps from one life transition to another, we will get to where we are supposed to go. We will frustrate ourselves if we expect too much personal change too soon. Keep your life-stage in clear focus. It's not necessarily bad for you to be where you are. All experiences can change you, not others. The experiences of life are yours. Don't waste energy or sleep over finding a more sophisticated tool for getting back at those who may have harmed you. Trying to get back at others, getting even, showing them, or blaming them will rob you of happiness and joy.

Relax. We develop our own character. We lived in an environment at school, at home, in church, and on the job with differing personalities. Life is only the environment. We are responsible for what we do with it. And we create the environment for our loved ones and others. We react to our environment and certain personality styles in our own unique way. Nobody made us the way we are. Stop whining. The good news is that we can change ourselves. Our changes do not depend on other people. We can change our automatic reactions to the atmosphere or context or environment that others created for us. We can relax into our own personality.

PRACTICE BEING FOREVER IN AN OPTIMISTIC STATE

People who are eternal optimists live in chronic joy. They may be labeled Pollyannas. That's really an honor. Remember the story. Everyone was depressed. People lived in gloom. The economy was horrid. Everybody hated their lives. Then came a girl named Pollyanna. Within weeks, people were chronically joyous. They started being kind to each other. Joy was in the air. Everybody took the step to being chronically in joy.

TAKE IN THE NOURISHING QUIET OF REST

Another step we can take is to rest. Imagine what difference we could make if we just spent one day out of each week in pure rest. That restfulness will not lead to joy if we use it to do errands or go shopping at the mall or go to the movies or a sports event. Rest is the needed step to restore our souls. Rest is not a sign of laziness or weakness, but restfulness is a sign of wisdom.

We are in such a hurry to succeed, to pack each moment with activities, that we don't leave ourselves time to enjoy, to reflect, to rejoice, and to be grateful, or for rest.

How much joy have we missed because we hurried? Don't let joy pass you by. Do we take time to notice as life slips away? When we take the step of rest, we don't miss out on joy, we find it. How many of us schedule time for restfulness? Leave the week behind and you will enter a refreshing plane of existence. Let us stop thinking about work. Don't even scribble out mental calculations, for that comes under the heading of more work. Rest does not restrict joy. Rest sets us free for more joy.

Rest leads to joy for we can be still, still enough to hear the things we often miss. In the stillness, the nourishing quiet, we will appreciate the gifts that we take for granted each day. Imagine what could happen if we let go of the cares of the week, if we could allow our bodies and souls to relax. Imagine living in the present and not fretting about the past or the future.

These steps to joy will spill over into the remaining days of hills and valleys. Days preceding the step of rest will be days of expectation and excitement. Even the most difficult valleys become tolerable when we know a day of peace and quiet is shortly arriving. Our other days will shimmer with the afterglow of a revived spirit. We will gain a completely different perspective on life's struggles. This step toward joy will allow us to give thanks, to heal, to reflect, and to face whatever lies ahead with a renewed calmness.

Now begin to think about how your changes will affect others. Will your attitude and behaviors create a new atmosphere for joy? We will sense new energy to see things from a new and enlarged point of view, perhaps ever re-evaluating perceptions of our own.

Observe yourself and how you tend to function in various environments and with different people. Check the accuracy of your hypotheses about other people and make the corrections you need to make. Don't postpone your joy.

WHAT IF WE COULD NEVER DIE?

Many of us fear death. We'll do anything or pay any price just to postpone death a few days. Suppose we could never die. What would that mean? The blind grandmother would remain blind. The paralyzed among us would never walk. Those with serious mental illness would never recover. The retarded child would never experience a normal mind. Everything in this world that is crooked would always be crooked. The injustice in our world would prevail. The last, the least would remain last and least. Terminally ill people would remain in hospice or hospital, but they would never terminate.

In this life there is never total healing. Lazarus finally did die. Suppose we could never die. That would be a disaster. Each of us deep inside desires a life not measured by years. We want to have another crack at life. Perhaps if we could do it again, we would do something differently. The Pennsylvania Dutch people have a saying, "Too soon old, too late smart." The struggle never ends in this life.

What if we would die and not be dead? Only then will our struggles end.

That is where joy begins.

FREE TICKETS TO A JOYOUS PLAY

Living is like being given free tickets to a joyous play. With each sunrise, the curtain rises and we experience another scene. But this succession of scenes cannot go on forever. An 80-year-old person sees 29,200 daily parts of his life play. But the scenes do not go on forever. And really it is as long a play as you'd want to review in heaven. Sooner or later even the most enthusiastic play-watcher would get bored and grow weary of the struggling times.

So what happens when we leave the theater? Is the stage as dark and blank as when it was before the life-play started? Or does some new form of awareness begin. Nobody has come back to tell us.

Most people believe something goes on after death. Perhaps it is naïve to think so. But the happiest people know it. If we each have trillions of brain cells, and if looking another way, we can see billions of universes. The whole thing is so complicated and so balanced, too well arranged to end in meaninglessness. Human beings do not cease after a change that removes the physical aspects of us. It's too beautiful and complex to not have a point.

PRACTICAL APPLICATION

Find ways to help you get in touch with the chronic joy instinct.

Suggestions:

1. Get your personal cheerleaders. Surround yourself with a network of joy touched souls, family, and friends. Limit your time with those with negative and critical attitudes.

2. Take care of emotional business. Address your past issues and messages that kill your joy instinct.

3. Live in the present. Learning to live in the present moment is a key to your path to jouissance. Go for it.

Life's Clock

The clock of life is wound but once
And no one has the power to tell
Just when the clock will stop
At a late or an early hour.

Now is the only time you own
Live, love, toil with a will.
Place no faith in tomorrow
For the clock may then be still.

We cannot see, we cannot know
The meaning of it all
Just why the road must winding be
Or why the tears must fall

But face to face one day with God
In Heaven's glorious land
The darkened glass will be removed
And then we will understand.

XIV

STARTLING CHRISTMAS JOY

It's joy in the air time, joy everywhere time, it's Christmas time.

— Linda Gail McReynolds

CHRISTMAS IS A JOURNEY TO JOY. "Joy to the world, the Lord has come." The problem is that joy cannot be bought, produced, sold, or stolen. There's no joy on discount at a department store. We can't buy joy in a cup. We can't download joy. We can't make laws for it. We can't seduce joy. We can't turn it on with our remote control. We can't earn it. And we can't inherit it. Advent is the journey; Christmas is the joy.

Christmas is a journey toward joy. But we are not so much the ones traveling to find it as we discover that joy comes toward us. So we cannot manufacture joy or produce it or control it, but we can build a way for it. If we build it, it will come. We create an atmosphere or an environment for joy to come to us.

Keep Christ in Christmas. We see these words on signs everywhere during Advent. With Christmas being such a source of joy even for poor, Scrooge-like people who never celebrate Christmas as a religious holiday, take in joy at that time.

More money is spent. More energy is spent to create joy

by giving surprises, Christmas parties in most every workplace, Christmas programs attended by people who never "darken the door of the church" except in the festivities of Christmas. Some people are so full of Christmas that they start buying presents at the beginning of October.

Where's the joy? Santa Claus is not the magic maker in a red suit. He works from nine-to-five each day to feed, clothe, and shelter the family.

December is usually a valley time for families. Frustration at not being able to experience or give joy triggers winter depression. Ice and snow, falls and automobile accidents, overspending on credit cards, and not seeing most of one's family cause people to experience the doldrums of Christmas, or go away on a cruise or attend a holiday basketball tournament just to get away from it all. Dark mornings come earlier. Little children are afraid of the Bogeyman. Some are the only ones awake during the dark.

Some kids are afraid of the dark. Not so much that they are cold, hungry, or alone, but that that loneliness and fear could be interrupted by the Bogeyman. We remember that the Bogeyman, or your own equivalent, waited until children were alone in the dark before the creature or person scared the wits out of them. Sometimes kids try to go to sleep before other members of the family. If our parents knocked on the door, which was usually the bedroom where all our siblings slept, we wondered if it was the Bogeyman.

A BOGEYMAN STORY

One little guy told of the dark December night when he used his two best defenses of being in the dark with his siblings and falling asleep first, the worst fear happened. A knocking on the bedroom window awakened him. It was not just a scraping limb or a gust of cold wind. It was an unmistaken knocking. One eye opened and then closed quickly. He did not want him to know he was there. But the thing kept knocking. He slid under the covers subtly so as not to give away his opossum performance. The Bogeyman continued to knock and call the boy's name.

The voice sounded a bit familiar. He decided to do what he feared most. He turned his head to face the window. Of course, he did it as a child tossing in his sleep.

When he opened one eye again, whatever was out there saw him. It said, "Son, don't be afraid." I opened my eyes wider and I saw him and my fears turned to joy.

"It's daddy. I forgot my house key. Will you let me in?"

THE EPIPHANY OF PASSIONATE JOY HITS US

Like most children, this joy stays in the head, especially when winter comes in December. And at Christmas, one remembers that the story of Christmas begins with fear and ends in joy. God comes for those who need God, not because they are poor or sick or unable to care for themselves.

When the extraordinary interrupts the ordinary it is impossible not to know fear. Stories of Christmas joy abound as we share the memories of our individual joy times. On Christmas morning the last gift is often not under the tree, but in a special place. Children jump up and down, squealing with excitement. The adults are already excited as they wait for the child's response to catch up with their own. Christmas is a season of joy.

Have you been there? Has your heart caught up with that of our Father who announced through angels, "Do not have fear! We have good news of intense joy for all people—for you!" Christmas is a special time for joy. The story of the birth of Jesus is at the root of ever family or personal celebration, tradition, regardless of their perceptions.

CHRISTMAS IN HISTORY

The word *Messiah* used in the Bible means an individual sent by God to change history. Messiah was to save humankind from their pain and suffering. The Greek translation for Messiah is *Christos.*

The world celebrated the birth of the Unconquered Sun in pre-Christian times. By adapting some of the joy-seeking festivals of the Roman Empire, the early Christian church movement, meeting in each other's homes, captured the joy-seeking spirit. Celebrating the coming of Christ brought them the most joy ever known. Christmas joy comes from the birth of the unconquered Son. For nearly four centuries, Christianity spread slowly. Christians celebrated their joy on different days and in different ways as people were converted from various lands and cultures.

When the Roman emperor Constantine was converted to Christianity, he decreed that December 25 would be the official day of celebration. Constantine had practiced a religion called Mithraism, which was the religion of thousands of Romans. When Constantine declared himself a believer in Jesus as the Christ, he left the practice of his old religion, but he decreed that Christmas would be celebrated on the day of Mithra's birth. Christmas and the days surrounding it were times of fun, laughter, festivals, feasting, dancing, and revelry. Constantine rightly had the perception that the best method of winning converts was not by forbidding people to celebrate Mithra's birth or the season of Saturnalia, but by turning these old traditions into a new joyful purpose of celebrating the bringing of joy into the world through the birth of Jesus.

Almost all pre-Christian cultures celebrated days of the winter solstice. These rituals were designed to get people through the dark, cold days of winter, the shortest days of the year. Christmas day was to bring joyful light into the darkness of winter. Jesus the Christ brought light into these winter days. Of course, Jesus was not born on December 25. But for nearly 2,000 years, this celebration has proven no more wonderful time to celebrate with days of Christmas joy. Christmas is a time to find your joy instinct.

CHRISTMAS IN THE BRITISH ISLES

During the Middle Ages, Christmas became the most popular holiday in the British Isles. Joy was expressed from kings to beggars. People quit work on Christmas day and gave themselves entirely to pleasure. And nobody has entered more heartily into the joys of the season than the Britons. The day was marked by plays and pageants and musical productions, much like the Christmas cantatas of today.

With the Protestant Reformation, British Christmas celebrations were transformed. Calvinists saw Christmas as more of a secular holiday that brought excuses for unruly behavior. Puritan rule brought darkness into the days of December winter. When the monarchy was restored, Christmas was again legal.

CHRISTMAS IN THE UNITED STATES

In the United States, the first state to legalize Christmas was Alabama in 1836. Most of the states had legalized Christmas as an official holiday by 1880.

We come together. We go home for Christmas. No other celebration gives us the vision of gathering around a tree before a fireplace as we share anew, with joy, each other's faces, and each year the faces mean more to us.

Some of us keep the Christmas balls and the decorations from years past to help us store the joys of Christmas. From poinsettias to mistletoe, from manger scenes to our Christmas trees, our traditional decorations continue annually to lift our spirits and remind us of the joy that has come into our world.

The first community in America to share a decorated Christmas tree was Pasadena, California, in 1909. The following year, Boston and New York added a public tree. Today, nearly every community boasts a tree of simple beauty in the town center to remind us of the joy of Christmas. The first indoor Christmas tree in the White House was completed by Franklin Pierce and his family. And not until 1920 did President Warren Harding see that a Christmas tree was decorated on the White House lawn.

Each year candles blaze in churches and homes all over the world to honor the birth of Jesus. Candles represent the hope that Christ might be guided through the darkness to our homes. Even non-Christians sense the passionate joy.

The Advent wreath with five candles represents each week before Christmas, and one—the Christ candle of white—is lit on Christmas day. Most families place a star at the top of the tree representing the star mentioned in Matthew's gospel. Many joyful memories are of walking around our towns singing

Christmas carols to the lonely, those in nursing homes, prisons, and "the least of these." In European countries, singing children walk through the streets in groups carrying a box containing small nativity scenes. Advent activities bring a passionate joy for people who have never known Christmas as a time for joy, but rather too often a time for depression.

Food is another happy and at times joyful heritage. The eating table is extended for family and friends. As children we are entranced by the energy put into the dinner meal with leftovers gladly eaten for a month. Only a slight whiff of a certain odor instantly triggers our videotapes of Christmas past in our heads to transport us back to those feasts at home with our family. Little children make sure Santa has something to eat as he visits their home. Cookies and milk have been favorite treats.

In the Netherlands, children provide for Saint Nick's white horse on Christmas evening. Kids in Holland stuff their clean wooden shoes with hay and carrots and place them on their colorful windowsills. A dish of water is placed there also. We have made Christmas a worldwide celebration by reading how others celebrate Christmas. Joys, whatever the time zone shall echo in the atmosphere for everyone in the morning as the surprises for Christmas day are shared with moments of joy. Charles Dickens's character Tiny Tim said it for us all, "God bless us every one."

Mary Jane Carr wrote, "Let your hearts be filled with joy, while Christmas bells are ringing." On street corners, at the shopping malls, in churches, on doorsteps, in the streets of neighborhoods, or inside by the fireside, people join together with music. Carols were created for common people to display their joy and happy spirits. Country music, seasonal ballets, oratorios, and moving hymns mark Christmas joys with each note echoing the song sung by angels to shepherds in fields.

Each song has a theme of joy. One of the first carols written by some unknown person in the fifteenth century after the Puritans had outlawed Christmas was titled, "The First Good Joy That Mary Had." It describes the joy of the mother of Jesus as she recognizes the divinity of her Son. In an old hymnbook placed in the Bristo Baptist Church in Edinburgh, Scotland, we find the words to this hymn said to have been sung with unrestrained joy:

> "The first good joy that Mary had . . . It was the joy of one to see the blessed Jesus Christ when he was first her son. When he was first her son, good man . . .
> "The next good joy that Mary had . . . It was the joy . . . to see her own son Jesus. Christ makes the lame to go, to make the lame to go, good man."
> And the chorus was: "And blessed he be, Father, Son, and Holy Ghost, to all eternity."

Handel wrote *The Messiah* during a time of manic joy. He composed the whole composition in a few weeks, an incredibly short time for such a beautiful work that takes more than three hours to perform. Handel's musical achievement has no equal in the world of music. Handel was never a religious person. But he was filled with God-intoxicated joy when he wrote *The Messiah*.

And we cannot imagine music for enhancing Christmas joy as does *The Nutcracker* by Peter Tchaikovsky. This ballet tells the story of a brother and a sister who receive some special and magical Christmas gifts. One gift was a nutcracker in human form. The children can't agree to share the nutcracker, and so they go to bed with the issue unresolved. In the darkness of night, the sister climbs out of bed to retrieve the nutcracker. She comes upon a fantasy scene of toys and mice in battle. The nutcracker commands the toy soldiers. They are losing the battle with the King of the Mice. The sister, named Clara, throws her slipper at the mouse leader and wins the battle for the toy soldiers. Her reward is a joyful journey with the nutcracker now transformed into a handsome prince. They go to a kingdom of sweets, where she meets the Sugarplum Fairy. The ballet then reveals a scene of beautiful colors and delightful dancing that has brought smiles to our faces for generations. Seeing a performance during the holidays can enable your passionate joy at Christmas.

BELLS RINGING OUT CHRISTMAS JOY

The grandest cathedrals as well as the humblest Christian churches have bells pealing out the happy news of Christmas. Bells have been part of the ministry of churches since the fifth century. Church bells were first clanged in Italy to call worshippers to worship. Saxon king, Egbert, decreed that all church services be announced by the ringing of bells. Church bells still chime daily, but at no time is their sound so clear or their ring as joyous as when they sound out in celebration of the Christmas miracle.

WHY TRUE CHRISTIANS ARE SO PASSIONATELY JOYFUL

Joy is the one most distinguishing identities of true Christians. When valley times came for the disciples, they showed human fear. Still nobody was sad around Jesus during his lifetime. During his infancy, Jesus and his family experience great terror, but they calmly left their home for Egypt. At age twelve when he told his parents he was about his Father's business, no-body showed sadness. When he told his disciples that he desired to see his joy inside of them—"that your joy may be complete"—it happened.

Those outside the faith could not understand that joy. The first Christians were not wealthy. They had no earthly power. Their wealth was one of joy. It was then and is now shared with a world starved for love and times of joy.

There was a stigma toward those who were called Christ-like or Christians. There were very few of them. Powerful people viewed them as a dangerous cult. Yet their joy was not to be contained. Perhaps jouissance is a better word for their joy.

The apostle Paul wrote of "joy unspeakable and full of glory." To the Christians at Ephesus, he said that Christians sang not routinely but from the overflow of their direct experience. Life was not a problem to be solved, but a mystery to be lived.

Joy was something new in the world that brought food for hungry souls. No longer were people in the world starved for love.

Today this happens in our own infancy and childhood. Our grandson shared this joyful experience when his mother's unconditional loving smile awakened him each morning. And as his coordination developed, he gave the gift of the flickering of his answering smile. This process continued into childhood. His mother did not teach by stern rules, threats, or exhortations; but joy took root as he accepted his mother's gift of the joy instinct. Mothers can pour in the love and love will come out of the joyful child.

Christmas brings out the joy. And nothing will ever happen to separate us from the infinite love of God. That is clearly our reason for joy.

Between the parties and the pageants, the stockings and

the stores, the quiet moments of startling joy and grace are over-looked. These simple moments in complicated, stressed lives will pull anyone in, bring a smile to the face, and remind those who have experienced it all their lives of the spirit of the season. Even those new to Christmas such as people in the Middle East sense a spirit of love, a mark of passionate joy. In all our experiences of celebrations in the world's many religions, nothing illuminates miracle moments in a messy world like Christmas.

CHRISTMAS JOYS REMOVES MOUNTAINS

We find stories of unbelievable and surprising Christmas joy in rare places. One mountain tale says that there was an old woman who lived at the foot of a tall mountain in the Blue Ridge mountain chain of Virginia. Her church was located on the other side of the mountain. Every Sunday and Wednesday nights, she drove her old beat-up beast of an automobile to attend services. The old car would choke and belch. Then the same sounds accompanied her ride back home. She even chanced driving in rain and snow. Others didn't even try to travel those roads.

One prayer meeting night, she told her pastor that she had prayed for the mountain to be moved. She was a praying woman and the people were convinced she had the ear of God, but this one prayer about moving a mountain, well it was not taken seriously by anyone.

One summer day the woman had the women's group meet at her house. When the ladies drove into her driveway, they saw some men with surveying equipment. They were curious so asked what those men were doing.

"We are from the state department of transportation," one

replied. "Before Christmas a new highway is scheduled to be built right across this way. We'll have to remove that mountain."

So if Christmas joy is going to get to us, we must create a way. Take the steps. Relax. Believe. Let go of the clutter, the roadblocks. Christmas is a time for joy.

PRACTICAL APPLICATION

Attend Advent or special Christmas celebrations. Light the Christ candle with your family. Share the meaning of Christmas with people in your world of work or the neighborhood. Passionate joy inhabits the worlds of plain people struggling with the problems of ordinary life. Find it in a quiet place in your community. It may not be in the stores.

Make time for pleasure during Christmas. Schedule some time for fun. Give yourself a healthy emotional escape from the cultural commercial Christmas concepts.

Fake it until you make it. Mary Kay used this phrase as inspiration. Practice holding your joy instinct at the times when you don't feel it. Condition your mind, body, soul, and spirit to receive and recognize the joy.

Attend some celebrations of your Jewish, Muslim, or other friends who view the world differently. Notice the passionate joy that they have from their life perspective. Share the joy that comes from not drawing a line in the sand but by genuinely embracing each other's passions.

XV

ETERNAL JOY

The average person who does not know what to do with this life wants another one which shall last forever.

— Anatole France

WHEN PEOPLE WANT TO READ about joy, there are few books published on the subject. Most every minister tries to write at least one sermon on joy, but most of them are poor products of tired, harried, and crabby preachers—definitely not joyful.

There's C. S. Lewis and *Surprised by Joy*. There is a small book called *True Joy: the Wisdom of Saint Francis and Clare*. We usually turn to the section called "True and Perfect Joy." We can skip through Francis's poems and prayers. And you won't miss much not reading his exhortations and salutations. Toward the end of the book, there is a story of Francis coming to the monastery in the middle of the night. Francis was cold, muddy, tired, and hungry. When he begged to enter, the guard said, "It's too late. Nobody comes in here at this time of night." Finally, Francis does not say something religious or saint-like. He just says, "If I had patience, and did not become so upset, there would be joy in this."

Joy has an eternal quality about it. Staying in the videos

on the shelf of your brain, memories of joy times stay with us forever. Joy is both subtle and boisterous. We might think of joy like water. There are droughts, and then it washes and sprinkles. Sometimes it floods. It is a transcendent, spiritual experience that awakens harmony, goodwill, and peace. Joy relates to times of success and achievement, but the most authentic joy comes from the simplest moments in our lives: holding hands, catching fireflies, listening to music, or watching a sunset. Joy is not a production or financial investment. Building a wealth of joy won't improve your bank account, but it will do wonders for your soul account. Joy is an open well inside our souls. We find it difficult to relax our minds to this truth.

INTERNAL AND EXTERNAL JOY

Internal joy is experienced inside ourselves. External joy is the joy that comes because we achieve what we desire. External joy is easier to experience in the short run, but it is fleeting. External joy comes and goes with whatever is happening in our environment. External joy is extrinsic because it comes from the outside. We are as powerless as children over this kind of joy. When the circumstances change, joy arises. When our fortune reverses, this level of joy leaves us. We can't make joy happen. Contingent joy appeals to us, causes us to believe the only joy that we can experience comes from trying to make it happen.

Saint Francis started his work on joy by explaining that "a messenger comes and says that all the masters in Paris have come into the Order; but you must write, this is not true joy."

In our era of time, Francis could have written: "You receive a phone call from a head hunter offering a job with a promotion and extensive increase in salary. This is not true joy. You buy a new car. It looks wonderful and drives like magic, but this is not true joy. You are accepted into Harvard or Vanderbilt, but this is not true joy."

These passing joys are reasons to celebrate and they do produce joy. But, as we have encountered each other through this book, we realize that some memorable joy experiences produce temporary, contingent external joy. External joy depends on our circumstances lining up in just the right order over and over again. And we know this does not always happen.

Internal joy is more of an eternal joy. It is more difficult to enjoy because we must choose it each day, actively not passively. Internal joy is what Francis called true joy. True joy happens when we live in the moment, opening the door to inspiration and meaning, especially during our days of suffering and pain. This true joy enables us to look to the future, to eternity with hope rather than anxiety. Internal joy springs from the interior world and its development. It helps us overcome our inner emptiness and to find who we are. Eternal joy leaves out the "x" factor of external joy. It is found in patience, in our realistic but irritating moments, and we are left to wonder why.

We can imagine in our inner minds Saint Francis, all cold and muddy, knocking on a gate and being refused entrance. Francis had to stand out in the cold. He experienced rejection. He had to stay wet, perhaps on an icy night in December, and take whatever would come. His comment was not, "Thank you for this life lesson." He said, "If I had patience, and did not become so upset, there would be true joy in this." Did Francis mean in suffering and pain? Internal joy is an experience that is deeper than external situations. Internal joy, *jouissance*, springs from within external situations and is grounded in profound awareness of both the joys and sorrows that are life.

Francis of Assisi tries to find joy in the midst of intense

discomfort, fatigue, and irritation. Khalil Gibran informs us that "the deeper that sorrow carves into your being, the more joy you can contain." Friedrich Nietzsche insisted that joy only exists with the knowledge of pain. So joy is not a negation of suffering and pain. Joy is a counterpart to sadness. And sadness affirms our joy. Suffering calls for authentic joy, because life was meant for joy. Can joy survive if our external environment shuts down all kindness, generosity, humanity, and all contingent or external joy?

Life is passionate, extravagant joy. It tells us that joy survives even intense deprivation and cruelty. Building a wealth of joy in a world starving for love can test the existence of joy. It is not impossible to celebrate amidst sadness and lack of love. Our love-starved world lives with outer emptiness and the potential for inner emptiness, yet still can build a wealth of joy. We can mix joy with our sorrow and create wholeness.

Swiss psychoanalyst Verena Kast insists that our world spends far too much time exploring anxiety, depression, guilt, and anger, and not enough time exploring joy and hope. At a Jungian conference in Zürich, she told us the more attention should be given to emotions, especially joy. A great deal is said about anxiety and rage. Shame and guilt receive much too much attention, as do depression and grief. Joy is seldom spoken of, in spite of the fact that a major concern of therapy is the individual's search for happiness and joy.

Kast goes even further. She believes that our world distrusts joy. We equate it with irresponsibility and mania. We view people who struggle with suffering and pain as unworthy or impossible. Some people, she said, have guilt about experiencing joy after the death of a loved one, or the inability to feel any pleasure when others in our world suffer.

We note that there is a vast difference between irresponsibility and joy. We are in fact irresponsible when we refuse excessive joy. We cheat ourselves and those who suffer. Those who suffer need joy so that they can remember that it is still there, perhaps asleep under their bed. And we will need their help when joy is asleep under our own. Gibran reminds us that joy and sorrow are inseparable. "Together they come, and when one sits alone with you at your board, remember the other is asleep upon your bed." His words offer comfort. Joy and sorrow walk hand in hand. And when we find sorrow, they remind us that joy is still asleep upon our beds.

If you feel happy now, or just experience joy, remember a hill or highlight is followed by a valley or lowlight. Go back and look at your life chart. None of us stays in the valley forever. And neither do we stay on the hill—at least not in this life. We must learn to sing the sad songs of life. We need certain skills to climb out of depression. Take medication, pray, or run ten miles when you are experiencing the enigma of anger and rage. Sing when you are happy. Laugh a belly laugh long and loud. Do a cartwheel just because you still can. Color pictures with your children or grandchildren with bright hues. Joy is not merely incidental to your life's quest. It is a vital vision quest for us all. Despite our world starved for love, we can open ourselves to the joy that lives within each of us. Without love it becomes difficult to recognize our own joy and giving it space to exist and grow. Make room dear ones. There is joy without and within. Make room for it to grow.

VIEWING THE WORLD IN THE EXTERNAL AND THE INTERNAL

Because we live in a world of physical form and we have a human body, it is easier to understand why we view the world from the outside instead of the inside. Our innermost thoughts affect our outside world. The world of cause and effect is based on the phenomenon that our thoughts are a cause that manifests as physical forms or effects over time.

Our physical world including our human bodies is made of objects whose building blocks are composed of atoms. Atoms are infinitely small positive, negative, and neutral energized subatomic particles. They whirl around at fast speed and great distance from each other in relation to their size.

There is much more empty space than there is solid matter in physical objects that surround us, including our human bodies.

Study stars in the night skies. They resemble the subatomic particles that comprise your body. There is much empty space between each star. That vastness between the stars in space is similar to the empty space between the subatomic particles in your human body.

Solid matter does not exist as we perceive it. Atoms consist mostly of empty spaces. Because atoms exchange their subatomic particles with each other, there is a physical connection between all objects. All of us are part of one inseparable web of interconnections of matter and energy.

According to all this scientific insight of the law of cause and effect, we attract what we think about, both positive and negative. If you would like more joy, think positively with a joyful anticipation. Resist fearful anticipation, and you resist fearful consequences.

Our outer world is a mirror of our inner thoughts. We can change our outer world by changing our inner world. Because our bodies have physical form, they are composed of matter that is limited by time and space. Time is defined as the period it takes a body or object to move from one point in space to another point.

Do our spirits have physical form? We think not. So the dimensions of time and space do not limit our spirit. Thus our spirit exists in the past, present, and future and has no boundaries of space, time, or knowledge.

Our thoughts are a cause. Thoughts cause our brains to secrete chemicals that influence our natural functions and abilities. Thinkers and philosophers throughout history have taught that happiness and enlightenment require that we align our thoughts in harmony with the universe, or God, so that this energy works for us.

In his struggles, Luke Skywalker in *Star Wars* was told, "May the force be with you." He was also instructed not to permit his anger to open him up to the dark side of the force. Swim in the direction that joy and happiness are flowing. Relax and flow with the eternal stream.

THE BARRIER AND THE PASSAGEWAY

Living and experiencing the hills and valleys of our lives in this world can be a barrier to the eternal quality of joy. The world with its sin, selfishness, misery, suffering, pain, and closed attitudes closes our doors to *jouissance*. The world is a barrier and at the same time the world is the passageway to joy. When joy is awakened within us, the world can become the place from which joy is communicated to every one of us everywhere.

To dance with joy is to find ourselves differing with our reasonable expectations. And we are often aware of our natural inclinations toward addictions to misery. So knowing joy for most of us must involve suffering. We are aware of this connection between eternal joy and times of suffering as we think about the problem of evil.

Christians recognize Jesus's passion, death, and resurrection as the archetypal pattern of the relationship between joy and suffering. This is so mysterious to most of us that we are not able to understand. We are attracted to suffering as tragedy, and to failure as a dramatic form. Countless volumes have tragedy as the theme.

Intense pleasure is said to come from intense pain. This is the foundation of a psychopathology known as masochism, which seeks pain for the pleasure it brings. But the suffering that most of us experience is not sought after. Perhaps the suffering with which most of us are concerned is not a sought after pain. It comes when our prayer of "let this cup pass from me" is answered contrary to our own desire.

All of us, and perhaps more religious people than we have thought, can become masochists, and we must be aware of masochism lurking in the personalities among those who need to be punished and who need something to torment themselves with. The final note in the music of our lives is joy, but many notes of suffering are experienced in everybody's life.

THE VISION OF SAINT FRANCIS

We have mentioned Saint Francis of Assisi and his vision that joy was everywhere and forever. Catholic historians say he bore the stigmata. Joy and affliction have a mysterious unity. Illness, especially mental illness, reveals that those who bear the pain and experience suffering will also know the excessive joys of living. This is why to know joy is to be vulnerable to affliction so that we are aware of the possibility of joy.

Saint Francis, or Francesco di Pietro Giovanni di Benardone, lived from 1181 to 1226. Most joy seekers have gained strength from his little poetic song, "Make Me an Instrument of Thy Peace":

> Lord, make me an instrument of thy peace.
> Where there is hatred, let me sow love;
> Where there is injury, pardon;
> Where there is doubt, faith;
> Where there is despair, hope;
> Where there is darkness, light;
> Where there is sadness joy.

His second verse can be sung in juxtaposition to a worship or meditation time.

> O divine Master, grant that I may not so much seek
> To be consoled as to console,
> To be understood as to understand,
> To be loved as to love,
> For it is in giving that we receive;
> It is in pardoning that we are pardoned;
> It is in dying to self that we are born to eternal life.

One sure indication that you have lost your joy instinct is that you are experiencing less cheerfulness, less positive affect.

Joyful people rejoice in their strengths, talents, and powers, and they do not compare themselves to anyone. Passionate joy causes us to not be intimidated by the strengths, possessions, and powers of anyone else. *Jouissance* is rejoicing in all that you are, all that you have, and all that you can be and from knowing God in an intimate way that leads you to action in building a wealth of joy for the world.

If you are not living or experiencing a joy, you may observe your long pouting face and a chip upon your shoulder. You probably find it difficult to smile. It's a burden for you to be genial. And you do not know God, for God is love and joy.

In St. Francis's request, to sow joy where there is sadness removes the illusion of woe created in the mind and spirit of those who think they know God but never have known God.

The terrible truth is that suffering that is the most horrid does not give the faintest hint of the possibility for joy. Suffering causes us one wide wound. That keeps many of us from becoming wounded healers. When we come upon such suffering in somebody, it is natural for us to flee, to be rude, crude, or indifferent. We try to explain it away, or if we can, just have the stigmatized removed.

In that deep Old Testament story of Job, there is no explanation as to why his suffering has befallen him. Job's acceptance of his plight without explanation unveils his integrity and authenticity. Job is understood as a real person. His friends are traditional cardboard figures. Job realizes that there are more things that are unknown in the world than there are things known and understood. With Job's accepting the unknown in faith, joy came savagely out of the whirlwind in the most intense time of his suffering. Job's story and the story of Jesus's death and resurrection become the happy ending within what looks like this present world order. Joy and suffering come to be regarded as opposites instead of the correlatives they really are, that is, different sides of the same coin.

Paul in the New Testament told us to give thanks for everything. Kierkegaard said that this possibility of giving thanks is part of the eternity of joy. He meant that we do not give thanks as a result of the way things go in life, for the way things go is contingent and uncertain. Life goes up and down, to the hills and down in the valleys. But we can actually thank God whatever happens to us, in the sense that nothing can make our loving and believing God cares for us pointless.

Our inward ability to always thank God is the excessive joy that is a gift to us. Nothing can take it away. Of course we live in a world with cause and effect. Our lives are lived within natural order. The beauty that natural order reveals results from the natural laws of cause and effect. As people living together on this earth, we are never immune from the law of cause and effect. Suffering enables us to realize that we are bone of each other's bone, and flesh of flesh because it is the same law of cause and effect which is responsible for joy and beauty and suffering and ugliness.

BUILDING THE WEALTH OF JOY

The deepest and most important change will come to our love-starved world to the degree in which individuals appropriate joy actions and responses within and around them. We are all interconnected. So if one of us has an appropriation of joy, that joy will have repercussions that will extend to all humankind.

For us to deny that fact is to deny the possibility of prayer, the connection to our creator, and to count things visible as the only reality. Public action in building a wealth of joy is easily observable. Spiritual things are beyond time and space. Do we doubt the action of an invisible God? Do we suppose that God can work only in our understanding and humble intelligence? God is still speaking. As the vision of the United Church of Christ is worded, "Never place a period where God has placed a comma." God does not change even if our sensibilities do. In that vision, God still works to change the world for the better by means of things not seen. God is still speaking, and we have a part in building a kingdom of joy, in which we can all be blessed or happy even in the valleys of our lives. Maybe joy comes even because of the valleys that come our way. Joy comes in when we have emptied our lives in the desert times where we are enabled to be still. Joy creates a highway through the valleys and even through the mountains of our lives.

HAVING FUN BUILDING A WEALTH OF JOY

Another thing Confucius said was, "To put our world in order, we must first put the nation in order. To put the nation in order, we must put the family in order. To put the family in order, we must cultivate our personal life; and to cultivate our personal life, we must first set our hearts right."

Building a wealth of joy is fun. And it depends on people like us who give in to our joy instincts. It depends on millions just like you. Building a wealth of joy in our love starved world means doing what we know. We can do it by practicing and thinking about good things more and more and more until the joy instinct rules the world. By thinking on these things our lives will be positive examples that others will follow. Feeling your positive energy, those without love, will desire what you have. Facts stressed and repeated over and over again with passion will stay in our memory banks. Whatever we teach or learn only one time is quickly forgotten. But things repeated tend to stay. We learned our alphabet and multiplication tables by our grade school teachers repeating them day after day in grade school. Repetition and the fun of learning enabled you to know them by heart.

Live in passionate joy and the world will be a richer place, a better place.

PRACTICAL APPLICATION

Take stock. Make a list of your positive traits and reasons why you are so loveable.

Spend some quiet time alone. Take time to get to know and appreciate yourself.

Take time to grieve losses. If you suppress painful feelings, you also reduce your capacity to feel positive feelings.

Send me (Dr. James Evans McReynolds, 404 North 4th Street, Elmwood, Nebraska 68349-6022; phone 402-994-2266, e-mail joyquest@windstream.net) notes on how this book has enabled you to create a passion for joy in your life. Or invite me to speak at your church, campus, business, or hospital.

NOTES ABOUT THE AUTHOR

James McReynolds and his wife Laurel are founders of Visionquest International. They provide spiritual encounters through local churches, hospitals, prisons, retreats, seminars, family enrichment, business, and civic presentations. "One day your preaching will be, as my positive thinking, a fresh vision for communicating Christian faith. Jim, I anoint you the minister of joy to the world," Norman Vincent Peale said during a School of Practical Christianity in Pawling, New York. Millions have read Jim's books, articles, printed sermons, and newsletters. Others have listened to his television and radio presentations. He serves as a Christian counselor and spiritual director. As a licensed mental health practitioner, he believes that "souls are made for endurance." He has served as a diplomat of the World Pastoral Care Center, on the pastoral care committee of the Baptist World Alliance, and prayer and spiritual formation task forces of the Cooperative Baptist Fellowship.

While serving as information specialist for the Sunday School Board of the Southern Baptist Convention, his portfolio included promotion of the programs of ministry, including National Student

Ministries. His prolific ministry to students has included speaking on more than 2,500 campuses throughout the world.

He has served local church staffs in ten denominations. He is a retired elder in the United Methodist Church. He's been listed in *Who's Who in the South and Southwest, Who's Who in Health Care, Who's Who in Religion, Who's Who in America*, International Men of Achievement, and the *Dictionary of International Biography*.

Pastor Jim's formal education includes a BA, magna cum laude, Carson–Newman College, Jefferson City, Tennessee; graduate assistant in psychology of religion, Baylor University, Waco, Texas; BJour, University of Missouri, Columbia; MREd, Midwestern Baptist Theological Seminary, Kansas City; ThD, Luther Rice Theological Seminary, Atlanta; LittD, Cardiff Theological College, London; MDiv and DMin, Vanderbilt University, Nashville; PhD in business administration, California Coast University, Santa Ana; PsyD, Graduate Theological Foundation, South Bend, Indiana which included studies at Notre Dame, Oxford, and Rome Universities. His dissertation at Oxford was "Integration of Joy in Clinical Family Counseling."

www.ingramcontent.com/pod-product-compliance
Lightning Source LLC
Chambersburg PA
CBHW031242090426
42742CB00007B/285